PLANE CRASH

D0841330

PLANE CRASH

Michael Diamond

REVIEW AND HERALD® PUBLISHING ASSOCIATION
WASHINGTON, DC 20039-0555
HAGERSTOWN, MD 21740

The author assumes full responsibility for the accuracy of all facts
and quotations as cited in this book.

This book was
Edited by Raymond H. Woolsey
Designed by Bill Kirstein
Cover art by Mitchell Heinze
Type set: 11 point Palatino

PRINTED IN U.S.A.

R & H Cataloging Service

Diamond, Michael James, 1946-
    Plane crash.

    1. Survival (after airplane accidents, shipwrecks, etc.)
2. Aeronautics—Accidents.
I. Title.
        629.13

ISBN 0-8280-0507-9

CHAPTER

1

Wow, this is great! Mike Chambers thought as he flew high above the ocean along the coast of California. Nothing he had ever seen could compare with the dramatic beauty around him. Mountains capped with clouds jagged into the sea. Lofty cliffs like many-towered sandcastles guarded the sandy coves dotting the coastline. Waves crested with white pearls washed the shores. He felt like one of the seagulls sailing on the wind currents off the cliffs.

I can almost smell the salty air, he mused. *And to think, heaven is going to be more beautiful than this. I won't need a plane to fly there.*

Mike knew that soon his flight would end and he would have to touch earth again. The sun was slipping down beyond the blue Pacific as he sailed on the winds of the sky.

It's taking longer than I planned. Mike looked at his instruments. *The head winds are slowing me down. I'd better extend my flight plan or they'll think I've crashed.*

"This is 2499 Juliet," Mike called on the radio to Oakland Flight Service.

"Go ahead, 2499 Juliet," a voice crackled above the roar of the engine.

"I need to extend my flight time one hour."

"What is your location?"

"I just turned inland from the coast, heading toward San Francisco Bay."

"Roger. Your flight plan is extended."

Like a host turning on the lights for a guest, the city turned on her evening lights to welcome Mike. His birthplace glittered in the waters as he flew over the Oakland Bay Bridge.

Now, how far to Novato airport from here? In the orange glow from his instruments, Mike checked the charts on the empty seat next to him. *About 30 miles north*, he calculated. *At 100 mph, I'll be there in about twenty minutes.* Mike pushed on the yoke, pointing the nose of his plane down from 8,000 feet at the northern part of the bay.

The sun was gone now and it was dark. Mike was only a student pilot; he had never flown at night before, and never on this long a flight or so far from home. Nervous and wide-eyed, he kept checking the charts and looking out the window, trying to spot runway lights.

Mike knew there was a huge hill next to the Novato airport, but he couldn't see it. A few weeks earlier a twin-engine plane had crashed into it in the dark.

"Remember that hill," a friend at work warned him the day before. "A dentist and three others burned to death on it. So could you!"

Mike switched on his landing lights, and the hill loomed out from the darkness. His hands tightened on the yoke. *Lord, help me to land safely.* He grabbed the mike, his knuckles turning white as he spoke: "This is 2499 Juliet, calling Novato tower. Come in."

Seconds passed in silence as he awaited a reply. *I need to know which direction to land from*, Mike worried.

"This is 2499 Juliet, requesting landing instructions. Come in."

No answer.

It's after seven o'clock, Mike thought, glancing at his watch. *Maybe the flight office is closed. Small town, small airport.*

Mike looked down on the airport. *Where is their wind-*

sock? he wondered as he circled. *That could tell me if I should land from the north or the south.* Mike searched intensely. *Can't see it. I've been fighting a head wind from the north all afternoon though, and I need to land into the wind. That means my approach should be from the south.*

Mike positioned the Cessna 150 accordingly. He flew lower and lower—2,500 feet; 1,500 feet—everything looked good; 500 feet—

Suddenly a twin-engined commuter plane appeared out of nowhere, coming straight at him. Mike's heart jumped to his throat. The plane's lights, huge belly, and thundering noise seemed to bear right down into his cockpit. *Left, Lord, left! Have him bank to his left!* Mike banked to his left. The commuter roared clear on his right.

Thank you, Lord, Mike thought, shaking. But now he was headed for that killer hill. He banked sharply to his right and cleared it. *Thank you again, Lord.* The hill must have hidden the commuter till the last moment, he realized.

"Hey, is that Mike's plane up there?" asked Alan, Mike's six-foot-three-inch brother, to the rest of his family, who were waiting for Mike on the ground. "I'll flash the lights from my Scout to signal him." Alan jumped into his four-wheel-drive vehicle.

But Mike didn't see his brother's lights flashing on the ground. He circled above, waiting for the commuter to land. Then Mike landed the same way. He taxied to the front of the airport's small terminal and turned off the engine. "Praise God, I made it," he said. He climbed out of the plane.

"Wow," Alan exclaimed, "that was close!"

"Sure was, son," Mike's father said, hugging him.

"I landed against the direction of the wind," Mike said. "I couldn't see the windsock."

"Well, we've been waiting here two hours," Mike's mother said, "and all the other planes landed the same way you just tried to."

Mike learned later that the winds died down after

dark, and so aircraft were starting to land in the normal direction for that field.

"I was praying for you," his mother said.

"Thanks, Mom," he replied. "I need all the prayers I can get."

"You must be hungry, Mike," his father said. "Let's go."

"Maybe it was premature for your instructor to sign you off on this long a trip," his dad said as they walked to the parking lot.

"Maybe so, but I'm here now. And I have to get back."

"Hope this isn't an omen for tomorrow's flight," Alan said. "It's a long 500 miles back to Southern California. Anything could happen."

"I don't believe in omens," Mike replied. "But I do believe in prayer. God will be with me."

CHAPTER

2

It was a hot August afternoon in New York. The damp heat flowed through the open window of the Smithtown High School administrative office.

"Are you sure you want to be a pilot?" Mike's guidance counselor asked.

"Yes," Mike told him. "Ever since I can remember, I've wanted to fly."

"You're entering your final year here at Smithtown, Mike," the counselor said. "According to your test results, you show a great deal of mechanical aptitude. Have you ever considered auto mechanics?"

"I like working on cars, but I love flying," Mike replied. He stared out the window, through a maple tree, into the blue skies.

"Your grades are very good in automotive," the counselor continued, studying the test results in front of him. "You qualify for the automotive training program." He looked over his glasses at Mike. "What do you think?"

"What does it entail?" Mike asked above the whirring of the small fan blowing in the corner.

"You'd go to your regular classes during the day, then in the afternoon you'd be bussed to Wilson Tech Automotive in Commack. If automotive is not what you really want, you could still go into flying after graduation."

"Could I take my '55 Chevy convertible instead of the bus? It's old, but it could make the daily trip all right."

"I'm afraid not. The school has a policy on that. But there are times when students do take their cars in to work on. It would have to be cleared with your instructor. Am I to take it that your answer is yes?"

"Sure, sign me up. I'm always interested in learning more about fixing cars."

Mike graduated that year with two diplomas, a high school diploma and an automotive technology diploma. But he was still more interested in airplanes than in cars. Soon after graduation, he got a job as a refueler at MacArthur Airport in Long Island, New York. After two months at MacArthur, he went to work for Grumman's Aircraft as an assembly riveter on the Gulf Stream II. Mike tried to save money to go to flight school, but he managed to spend it all on his car or on alcohol.

After work he would get together with friends. They'd work out with weights, drink at a local bar, go to car races, or do a little racing themselves.

"Hey, Mike!" Johnny shouted to the driver of the car next to him. He raced the engine of his 289 Ford on the lonely piece of highway. "When that light turns green, you'll be eating my exhaust!"

"Oh, yeah?" Mike shouted back above the roar of the engines. It was Saturday night. "The smoke from my tires is going to blind your eyes!"

"The loser buys drinks!" Johnny shouted back.

"Well, I hope you have money!" Mike laughed, his eyes fixed on the light.

The light changed and Mike nailed his foot to the pedal. Tires screamed. Engines roared and Mike pulled away with his 283 Chevy, beating his friend.

While they were settling their drinking bets in the local bar, another friend, Jimmy Carney, walked in.

"Hey Mike, when are you coming over to the house to work out?" Jimmy asked through the smoky haze.

"Monday night," Mike answered, leaning back and

tipping his chair up on two legs.

Weeks and months went by. Mike worked out with Jimmy, and they also worked on their cars in Jimmy's barnlike garage, which was nestled in the woods away from Jim's house.

One cold Saturday night in February, when Jimmy was in upstate New York, Mike went to the garage alone to finish work on his new, red Triumph convertible. While he was under the car on his back, the jack holding it up slipped and the car fell, pinning him down.

"Ugh," Mike grunted as the weight of the car pushed the air out of his chest.

The frame lay across his chest. His head, shoulders, and arms were under the car; his lower torso and legs stuck out. *Thank God, it's my TR3 and not my Chevy!* he thought.

He struggled to get his arms into a position of leverage so that he could brace the frame and relieve the pressure on his chest, maybe even slide out. It didn't work.

What now? he thought.

"Hey!" Mike yelled. "Can anybody hear me?"

Nobody's even here, he thought to himself. *There weren't any lights on at the house when I drove by. And even if someone were there, they couldn't hear me at this distance.*

The damp cold was getting to him. He began to think about God and his own lifestyle.

I know I've ignored you, God, Mike prayed, *living for myself. But if you help me now, I'll go back to church.*

Then Mike paused. *What kind of bargain is that? Whom do I think I'm kidding? I won't go back to church. But Lord, I still need help!*

Suddenly Mike saw headlights flash under the closed barn doors. He heard a car door slam and saw, from under the car, someone sliding the barn door open.

"Jimmy, is that you?" a friend asked when he saw Mike's legs sticking out from under the car.

"No, it's me—Mike. Is that you, Mark?" Mike recognized the voice.

"Yep. What you are working on under there?"

"Nothing! I'm stuck. The jack slipped."

"You're kidding!" Mark exclaimed.

"I wish I were. It's been a long hour. Can you get this thing off me?"

"Sure!" Mark hoisted up the side of the car and Mike slid out.

Mike was surprised. "Hate to say it, but I didn't know you were that strong, Mark. You lifted that car pretty high pretty easily. By the way, what are you doing here? I thought you were supposed to be away at college."

"Just a weekend break. Where's Jimmy?"

"Out of town."

"Oh," Mark said, walking back to his car. He got in and drove off.

Mike finished working on his car, conveniently forgetting God and his prayer. But a few months later Mike ran into Mark again.

"Hey, welcome back, Mark. By the way, I never thanked you for lifting that car off me."

"What car?" Mark asked.

"You know, Mark. When you came home for a weekend last semester. You stopped by, looking for Jimmy, and found me in his garage under that TR3."

"What are you talking about?" was Mark's surprising response.

"Mark, you were there! Booze is destroying your memory cells!" Mike laughed and walked away. But then he remembered his prayer that night. "No," he said, shaking his head.

A few weeks later, Mike stopped by the pub where Jimmy worked part-time, bartending.

"What can I get you, Mike?"

"Make it a Seven and Seven," Mike answered looking around the packed room. "Look at these guys sitting around drinking away. Wasting their lives."

"You drink too, Mike. What's the problem?"

"Jimmy, we have fun driving around, going to the

Hamptons, Greenwich Village, watching the girls at Robert Moses Beach, waterskiing in the Long Island Sound. But you know what?"

"What?" Jimmy answered, toweling a glass dry.

"We're miserable."

"Oh, come on, Mike. Speak for yourself. We're having fun."

"Not really. We laugh a lot when we get together and drink, but there's no peace."

"That's why we drink!"

"There must be more to life than this," Mike insisted.

"Don't worry about it. Life is short."

"I don't know how short it is," Mike said. "The way I was taught, there is a God and a hereafter."

"Hey, enough of this. The next drink is on me," Jimmy poured another glass.

"Thanks," Mike responded. "By the way, I'll be away next week."

"Where?" Jimmy asked. He mixed Mike's drink.

"My sister is getting married to a minister's son in Lancaster, Massachusetts. It's only a weekend thing. I'll be back Sunday night."

"Preacher's kid, huh?"

"Yeah, Seventh-day Adventist. My sister and I grew up in that church, off and on. So when she went to college she chose Atlantic Union College. It belongs to the church."

"See you when you get back," Jimmy said.

The Friday before the wedding, Mike, his mother, and his younger brother, Alan, drove to the little Massachusetts town. Little did Mike know that it would be the beginning of a whole new life for him.

"Mom," Mike said as they sped along the freeway, "you must be excited about visiting California." She was planning to go there with relatives after the wedding.

"It's been 15 years since we left," she replied as Mike slowed to pay a toll. "I always hoped to take you kids back before you grew up. Maybe someday you'll get back to where you were born and see the towns you lived in."

"Which ones?" Mike asked, trying to picture them in his mind.

"You know, San Francisco, Richmond, Fresno, and a few others."

· "Yeah, I know. Which relatives are you going with?"

"You remember your cousin Lynne Dymott, from California, don't you?"

"Sure do. Five years ago she came with Grandpa and Grandma to visit with us at our old house in Brentwood."

"Lynne married a seminary student, Paul Eagan. They are both going to Debby's wedding."

"What's a seminary?" Mike asked.

"Paul is planning to be a Seventh-day Adventist minister and a seminary is where they train after college. The Adventist seminary is in Berrien Springs, Michigan."

"To each his own," Mike said. "As for me, I just can't wait till this wedding thing is over so I can get back home."

When they arrived in Lancaster, they drove to the home of Debby's in-laws-to-be.

"Pastor and Mrs. Remick, I'd like you to meet my mother and my brothers, Mike and Alan," Debby said.

Mike's mother spotted Paul and Lynne in the corner of the crowded living room. "Let's go over there, Mike. I want you to meet your cousins."

Mike shook Paul's hand and gave Lynne a hug. They talked about Lynne's visit five years earlier, and about family back in California whom Mike didn't even remember. His parents had moved to New York when he was 6 years old.

Saturday came and all went to church; on Sunday was the wedding.

"Well, Mom," Mike said during the reception. "Let's get your luggage and pack it in the Eagans' car."

"What's the hurry?" his mother asked. The reception was winding down. The bride and groom had just left.

"Alan and I are anxious to get started back. We don't want to get in too late."

"Okay, just a minute." His mother looked around for Paul and Lynne. "There they are," she said, spotting them across the reception hall, by the punch bowl.

"Well, Aunt Doris," Lynne said as they approached, "ready to go?"

"Just about. Can you come by the dorm where we are staying, to pick up my baggage?"

"Someday I'm going to go to California too," Mike told Paul and Lynne, "but right now I just want to get out of here." He turned to his mother. "Let's get you packed."

"Why don't you come with us, Mike? Come to California right now!" Lynne exclaimed impulsively.

"Are you kidding?" Mike laughed. "I do have a job to think about. Besides, I only packed for this weekend, not for a month."

"So what?" Lynne replied. "We'll go to laundromats more often. Come! We've got room in the car."

"Go ahead," Alan said. "I can drive back alone."

"Well, if you're crazy enough to ask me, I'm crazy enough to accept! California, here I come!"

The next morning the four of them started the long drive to California. As they traveled, Mike had time to observe his new cousin Paul. He noticed a peace in Paul that was compelling. Mike certainly didn't have it, nor did any of his friends in New York.

After many miles on the road, Mike said, "You know what bugs me? Christians think that they are better than the rest of us."

"Unfortunately, some do think that," Paul said, steering the blue four-door LeMans down the open highway.

"You admit that?" Mike was surprised.

"Sure," Paul answered. "But it's not a true Christian attitude. A real Christian acknowledges his source of goodness-God."

Once in California, Mike's mother stayed with her own mother and Mike traveled on with his cousins. Part of

Paul's seminary training involved working with an evangelist in Hayward, California. All three of them stayed at a church member's home.

Every night, Mike attended the evangelistic meetings with Paul and Lynne. He heard sermons on God's love and soon coming. But not until the final night was he convinced about his own need for God as his personal friend. For the first time, Mike heard an altar call.

"God loves you very much," the minister declared, his voice echoing in the large auditorium. "He wants to come into your life, to end your loneliness, to become your friend."

The room was quiet except for the minister's voice. "Bow your heads in prayer," he instructed. "If you want to give your heart to Jesus, come up here."

Mike glanced around to see if anyone was going forward. He felt uncomfortable. *That doesn't apply to me*, he thought. *I'm pretty good basically. I don't hurt anyone.* But suddenly, like a set of cymbals banging together deep in his soul, he seemed to hear, *Mike, go up!*

What? Mike responded, startled. *Not me! This is for sinners. Not me!*

Mike, go up, he heard again, this time more like a whisper.

No! Mike said as the minister continued to invite people forward. *It's not for me!*

Mike, go up. The voice was relentless.

Is that God calling me? Mike wondered in surprise.

He reached a decision. *I'll do it.* But when he tried to get up, his body felt like 300 pounds of lead. *I can't move.*

But the voice still called. Mike rose quickly and walked forward.

Suddenly, a river of peace flowed over him. He felt warmth he'd never felt before, to his core. He felt the peace he longed for. Things that once seemed important —alcohol, rock music, racing—suddenly lost their appeal.

After the meetings at Hayward, the three got together again with Mike's mother and started driving back east.

Paul and Lynne planned to drop Mike and his mother off at O'Hare Airport in Chicago, where they could catch a flight to New York. Paul and Lynne would continue north to Berrien Springs, Michigan, where Paul would continue his seminary training.

"Mike," Lynne said as they left the golden California hills. "What are your plans once you get back to New York?"

"Work at Grummans. Save up for flight school. But, come to think of it, I may have a problem at Grummans. I took off on this trip without letting them know. If they don't take me back, I'll just look for another job."

"The reason I'm asking," Lynne continued, "Paul and I would like you to stay with us in Berrien Springs. You could work there to save money for college. You could live with us for the final year we have to go. What do you think?"

"Wouldn't that put you guys out?" Mike responded. "Your place there has only one bedroom."

"Don't worry about that. We can get another place that has two. Come and be with us."

"Paul, is this your feeling also?" Mike asked.

"Sure is," Paul answered. "Getting tired of doing dishes." He laughed. "We can't afford a maid. You'll be the closest thing to it."

"If you're sure about this, okay. I've got some business back in New York I have to take care of first. And I'll need to get my clothes and my car. Give me a week. I'll drive back with my Triumph."

"Great! That will give us time to get the place ready for you."

"Mike, you're back!" Jimmy said as he opened his door. "I'd call that a lo-o-o-ng weekend. Some people would even call it a month."

"Jimmy, I have something to tell you," Mike said as he walked in. "I received Christ."

"Let's have a beer and you can tell me all about it," Jimmy headed for the refrigerator.

"No, thanks," Mike said, sitting down at the kitchen table.

"You haven't given up drinking, have you?"

"I just don't need it anymore," Mike responded as Jimmy sat down.

"Don't tell me you've become one of those!" Jimmy exclaimed in mock horror. He gulped his beer. "I grew up going to church. I heard dry and boring sermons every week. I'm a pretty good guy. I don't need it anymore."

"It's not a church that I received in my heart, but Christ," Mike responded. "I've heard some boring sermons myself, but Jesus isn't boring. He's exciting and so is life."

"What do you mean by that?" Jimmy asked.

"I have peace that I never knew before. A peace greater than anything I could have imagined. I don't need drink anymore. In fact, I don't need a lot of things anymore; they were just substitutes for what I really craved. What I thought was my own goodness looked pretty shabby next to real goodness. Christ showed that during His time here on earth. I'm a sinner, all right. But the good news is, He has the power to implant His goodness in me. That's exciting—to be healed of sin!"

"Well, Mike," Jimmy said over his glass of beer, "I do see a peace about you that I haven't seen before. But it's not for me."

"Yes, it is, Jimmy. I'll keep you in my prayers."

Mike's life was changing. Not only did he have a new life in Christ and start college, but he also met his future bride-to-be, Ann Louise Jones, at Andrews University. Less than a year later, they were married at Mission Inn in Riverside, California.

CHAPTER

3

Birds danced on the dewy morning lawns as Mike walked out of Loma Linda University Medical Center after his nightshift in security. *What a day!* he thought, crossing the campus to Ann Louise's office. *This is California at its best—palm trees, flowers, bright sunshine. God's beautiful creation. Wow! It's going to be a great day to fly to San Francisco.*

"Is Ann Louise here?" Mike asked Linda, the secretary at the Academic Publications office.

"Yes," she said, not looking up from her typing. "Go on in."

His wife was on the phone. Sitting down, he looked around. The morning sun beaming through the window above her desk spotlighted her degrees on the wall—Bachelor of Arts in English, from Andrews University; Master of Arts in English Literature, from the University of Redlands.

"How's the editor?" Mike asked when she hung up the phone. She looked up with a smile that could melt snow. "You look refreshed, as if you had slept the whole night through," she commented.

"I'm just excited about flying up to San Francisco today. Can I have the car keys?"

Ann Louise reached for them. "What about your classes?" she asked, handing them over.

"It's quarter break. I'm off until Monday. That's four days free. Good time for me to get my flight hours in. Elaine is going to raise her rental rates Friday. If I get in my last solo flight requirement for my pilot's license now, I'll save money. I'd like to see Alan and my folks too."

"That would be nice! You haven't seen them in quite a while." Ann Louise glanced at her day's work on the desk. "How are we going to work it out for me to have the car while you are gone?"

"Can you take an early lunch?"

"Sure."

"Once I've finished everything at home, I'll give you a buzz. Maybe your secretary could drive you home. Then you could drive me to the airport and keep the car."

"How soon will that be?"

"An hour or so. I'll change, then go to the airport to have my flight chart checked, then go back home to pack. I'll call you then."

Wonder where she parked today, Mike thought, scanning the parking lot and loosening his tie. *There it is,* he said to himself, spotting the trim orange Honda Civic. Mike slipped his sky blue security blazer off and folded it on the car seat beside him.

I hope I can use one of Elaine's planes today, Mike thought as he steered the car onto the freeway. This time the weather was good, not like three weeks ago when he had tried to make the trip.

At home, he put on his jeans and pulled a heather-blue turtleneck sweater over his head; then he ran a comb through his thick, dark hair.

"Elaine," Mike said, squeezing the phone under his chin as he tied his hiking boot laces. "Would one of your Cessna's be available for me to use today? I'd like to finish my cross-country flight hours. I'd be gone overnight and come back tomorrow, late afternoon."

"Sure," she replied. "Where do you want to go?"

"San Francisco."

"Fine." Elaine glanced at the aviation clock on the

wall. The propeller-like hands pointed to 11 o'clock. "How long will it take for you to get here?" she asked.

"Ten minutes to show you my chart. But then I'll need to come back home to pack. It would be an hour or so before I'd take off."

Dust billowed around the car as Mike turned onto the dirt road leading to FlaBob Airport. Driving past an old wooden hangar on the left, he approached a trailer with a sign on it reading, "Elaine's Flying Service." Beyond, he saw rows of old wooden hangars lining both sides of the road.

"Have you completed your chart?" Elaine asked Mike as he walked in.

"Yes, here it is, but I want to double-check it." Mike spread it out on the glass display case filled with the latest books on flying.

"I see you mapped out your route on a WAC [World Aeronautical Chart] instead of on sectionals," Elaine commented.

"Yes. Is that all right?" Mike asked.

"Sure," Elaine answered. The phone started to ring. She raised her voice—"It will be easier to handle in the cockpit than trying to coordinate two sectionals." (Unknown to Mike, the Federal Aviation Administration —FAA—requires student pilots to use sectionals because of the greater detail.)

Elaine spoke into the phone as Mike walked out. "May I help you?"

Mike went to the edge of the airfield behind the trailer and sat down at a small wooden picnic table. He opened his chart. A giant eucalyptus tree filtered the morning sun rays onto the table.

I'll be flying northwest from Riverside to the coast, and then north to San Francisco, Mike noted, looking at his plotted lines. *The Central California route would be scenic as well.* He pictured in his mind the Mojave Desert, with its dry dusty mountains looming from the tumbleweed floor, and the Tehachape Mountains, with pines reaching to the sky.

21

Then the San Joaquin Valley, with its rows of citrus trees, cottonfields, and the grapevines in Selma. *Maybe I'll fly back down that way tomorrow. Today I'll stick with the coastal route,* he decided.

"I think I'm ready, Elaine," Mike said as she walked by.

"Call the weather station," she said, "and write out your flight plan."

"How do I do that?"

"You don't know?" she asked. A Piper Cub roared in takeoff behind them.

"I haven't had ground school yet," he reminded her. (Ground school is not required by the FAA in order for a student to solo.)

"That's right," Elaine said. "A flight plan gives information about a trip. You file it with the nearest FAA flight service station, usually at the nearest international airport. In our case, the nearest station is Ontario."

"What's the procedure?"

"I'll get the form. Just a minute," Elaine turned back to her office.

"Here," she said, placing the form on the table. "Fill in the blanks. What is your hours-of-fuel time?"

"According to my calculations, I have over four hours of fuel."

"Put down that you have only three hours. Always allow yourself a margin, at least an hour. Now write down your refueling stop."

"That will be San Luis Obispo, my halfway point."

"OK, write down your destination."

"Novato," Mike said.

"Write down your aircraft—Cessna 150; and color —red and white. Then your ETA [estimated time of arrival]. What time are you planning to leave FlaBob?"

"About one p.m. That should put me in Novato around six, well before sunset.`

"When you write down your flight time, add at least an hour to it."

"Why?" Mike asked. A gust of cool March wind rippled his chart.

"Because you might have a head wind that would slow you down. You wouldn't want to be in the air when they think that you should be on the ground."

"Shouldn't I take the head wind into account when I calculate my ETA so I'll know exactly when I'll arrive?"

"Don't bother. I never do. Just add additional time to your flight plan to compensate for it," she answered. Nearby, a gas attendant climbed a small stepladder to top off the fuel tanks of a Cessna 172 next to the taxi strip.

"But what if I arrive after sunset?" Mike asked. "You haven't checked me out for night flying yet. I've never flown in the dark before. I'd hate to risk landing at an unfamiliar airport at nightfall."

"Don't worry. You'll get there before sundown." The smell of gas fumes drifted over as the attendant finished filling up.

"Okay, I've got the form filled in. What's next?"

"Call it in to the flight service station by phone. Once you take off, call them again on your radio to open your flight plan. After you land at your destination, call once more to close it. This is to let them know you arrived okay."

Mike followed her back into the office to make the call to Ontario Flight Service, then he called the weather station. "It's clear all the way, Elaine," he told her.

"Good!" she responded. Approaching footsteps interrupted them. Another student came in.

"I'll be with you in a moment," Elaine told the other student.

"Elaine, I do plan to fly back tomorrow," Mike continued, "but if something comes up so that I can't, would that be a problem?"

"Actually, yes. The plane is reserved for rentals all day Friday." She laughed. "I've only got two planes. That's how I make my living, you know."

"Okay, I'll do my best to get it back tomorrow. What

route is the fastest in case I get a late start—the coast or the inland valley?"

"Each is about 500 miles," she replied. "Decide when you get there and make up another flight chart then. Call me collect if you have any questions." (Again, unknown to Mike, flight instructors are supposed to check their students' route charting for the entire trip before releasing them for solo cross-country flights, not just the first leg.)

"I won't be here when you take off," Elaine said. "I'll leave the keys to the Cessna with the gas attendant."

The wheels of Mike's car spun the dirt on the road in front of Elaine's office as he hurried home to his little two-story condo in Riverside.

Mike phoned Ann Louise. "I'm home. Can you come now?"

"Be there in a few minutes."

"Aren't you worried about Mike flying such a long distance?" Ann Louise's secretary asked as they drove toward Riverside.

"I just won't think about it. He's so excited about flying that he's very conscientious about following all the proper procedures. I have to leave him in God's hands."

"Well, if I were married I would worry," Linda said as they drove down the freeway. "Mike must like heights."

Ann Louise laughed. "It's funny you should say that. Do you know where he took me on our first date?"

"No, where?"

"It was back at Andrews University, in Michigan, on a weekday night, when most students were studying. Mike called me up at the dorm and asked if I would be interested in climbing the campus water tower."

"What?" Linda questioned, raising her eyebrows. She glanced at Ann Louise. "You didn't do it, did you?"

"I agreed to on the phone, but when we met by the tower I had second thoughts. It looked so tall! But Mike reassured me so up we climbed. The steel ladder was icy cold. He loves the view from high spots. And flying is even better than a water tower!" They laughed.

"How long have you been married?"

"About three years. By the way," Ann Louise noticed, "it's the next exit."

"Thank you," Linda acknowledged. "Where is he from?"

"Mike was born in California, but grew up in New York."

"So he got his degree at Andrews also?"

"No, he took only a quarter there, but since then he's completed an associate arts degree here at San Bernardino Valley College. Now he's working on his industrial arts degree on the La Sierra campus and taking aircraft mechanics. He wants to be a missionary pilot for the church."

"What do they do?" Linda questioned as they drove off the freeway.

"They deliver supplies and medical personnel to remote areas of the world. He loves flying and he loves helping people."

Mike grabbed an apple from the kitchen and dashed up the stairs.

I'll just be gone overnight, he thought. *I won't need much.* He put a change of underwear and his shaving gear into a small suitcase.

"I'm home," Ann Louise called as Mike was about to close the suitcase.

"How about your wet suit jacket?" she asked as she walked into the bedroom.

"Wet suit!" Mike exclaimed. "I'm going flying, not scuba diving."

"But, sweetheart," she persisted. "If you get into trouble over the ocean and need to ditch, the wet suit jacket could keep you afloat and warm."

"That's the silliest thing I ever heard of! Sure, while the airplane is crashing I'd have time to unpack my suitcase and put the wet suit on, right? Or maybe I should wear it on my flight with my mask and flippers!" Ignoring Mike's protests, Ann Louise got the wet suit jacket out of the closet and handed it to him.

Oh, well. To keep her happy I'd better take it, Mike thought, and in went the wet suit jacket.

"I'd better call Alan to let them know that I'm on my way. I want them to pick me up at the airport."

Fifteen minutes later they drove up to Elaine's locked-up flying school. "She's gone all right, just as she said," Mike noted. Then he looked toward the gas pumps. "There's the plane over there."

"Here is my parents' phone number," Mike said, jotting it down for Ann Louise. "If anything comes up, give them a call. As soon as I arrive, I'll call you."

"Hey, don't worry," Mike said, noticing that Ann Louise had become quiet. "I'll be all right. And I'll be back tomorrow."

"Let's pray," Ann Louise responded. As was their custom before long trips, they bowed their heads.

"Lord," Ann Louise prayed, "we know that You love us very much and I pray that You will be with Mike during his flight and bring him back home to me. Amen."

"I love you," Mike said, squeezing her hand. "Well, this is it. Better get started." He got out of the car and shut the door. Then he leaned down to kiss Ann Louise through the open window. "Hey, are those tears?" he asked.

"Of course not," she said, but her smile was shaky. "Where can I watch you take off?"

"Drive further down this dirt road and make a left at the airport diner." As she drove away, Mike walked over to the gas pumps.

"Here are the keys," the gas attendant said. "The plane is fueled and ready."

"Thanks," Mike responded. "Just need to do my pre-flight checking and I'll be ready to go."

"Okay, Mike. Have a good flight. See you tomorrow."

Mike walked around the plane. *Looks good*, he thought, moving an aileron up and down. He checked the other ailerons and the elevator the same way. He opened up the oil flap cover on the side of the cowling to check the oil level. *It looks good too*, he thought. *Everything looks ready to fly.*

Preliminary checks done, he squeezed his six-foot body into the little cabin of the Cessna 150. *These seats aren't made for a 200-pound person*, he complained to himself. Then he looked at the empty seat beside him. *I wish Ann Louise could go with me.*

He started the engine and taxied to the beginning of the runway. He pressed down hard on the brake pedals and increased the engine speed to 2,500 rpm. Then he switched off the magnetos one at a time to check if the engine rpms dropped more than 100. All the magnetos looked good. All the gauges were in working order. He set the altimeter gauge to the altitude of FlaBob, 1,800 feet.

I'm ready! He checked for other traffic, then turned down the runway and opened the throttle wide. The plane rumbled down the bumpy asphalt. He raced by a few old biplanes tied down on the grass by the side of the runway. Excitement ran through his body like electric currents. The old 1950s diner flashed by on the right and the wheels left the runway. He glanced back to see Ann Louise but the afternoon sun cast a glare on the car's windshield and robbed him of seeing her. But as he became airborne, her last smile for him etched a picture in his mind.

"This is 2499 Juliet calling Ontario," Mike said into the mike as he climbed.

"Go ahead, 2499 Juliet," the tower answered.

"I'm calling to open my flight plan."

"Roger, your flight plan is opened."

He was on his way. His heart raced with excitement. He thought ahead to what he would soon see along the beautiful coast of California—sandy beaches, glittering ocean, rocky shorelines, crashing surf, steep cliffs. And then the Golden Gate Bridge and his loved ones.

Flying is easy. There is nothing to it, he thought. *I can't understand why three of Elaine's students crashed in mountains in the last year and a half. Two of them were killed*, he remembered somberly. One survived, but the plane was totaled. *I'm not going to be the fourth*, Mike determined as he climbed into the cloudless blue sky, his spirits rising with the plane.

4

B*eautiful!* Mike thought as he flew northwest over the valleys and mountains to the coast. The day was sunny and crystal clear. Cities and towns spotted the valley below, cradled by the surrounding mountains. Glass-towered buildings glittered like precious cut crystals. To his right were snow-capped mountains and to his left, beyond the valleys, the Pacific Ocean.

A few hours later Mike spotted a little town that looked familiar. *Where have I seen that place before?* he wondered. *Oh yes, it's Santa Paula, where Elaine and I flew for my round-robin cross-country flight. It feels good to be on my own.*

He checked his progress. *My halfway point for refueling should be coming up soon.* He compared his charts and his instruments. *Speed, 110 knots; altitude, 8,500 feet; heading, 335 degrees. Another hour to go.*

An hour later he spotted the San Luis Obispo airport and started in for his approach. He touched down and taxied up to the gas pumps.

"Top off the tanks," Mike told the young attendant in jeans and a plaid shirt.

"What time do you close the pumps?" Mike shouted above the roar of a twin-prop plane taking off. "I might stop by here tomorrow on my way back."

"Around five," the attendant shouted back.

Once refueled, Mike climbed aboard and took off. He

reached the coast about 30 minutes later and changed his course north to San Francisco. After his precarious landing at the Novato airport and meeting his family there, Mike went to his brother Alan's home for the night.

The first thing he did was call Ann Louise.

"I'm here, honey, safe and sound."

"Praise God," she replied.

"I did have a bit of a close call at one point."

"What happened?

"A commuter plane and I tried to land at the same time on the same runway."

"Wow. I'm glad you're all right."

"Me too."

"Well, get a good night's sleep. I'll bet you're bushed."

"I am and I will. It's been a long day and a long flight. I'll be glad to get home tomorrow. I love you and don't worry about me."

"I love you too. Be careful. I'm praying for you."

"It's good to see you guys," Mike said to Alan and his new wife, Lynne. Turning to Lynne, Mike commented, "Who would have thought, when we first met back in our old neighborhood in New York, that you would be Alan's wife and my sister-in-law!"

"Yeah," Lynne responded. "It's funny how things work out."

The phone rang. "It's for you, Mike," Lynne said, "your mom."

"How about breakfast with us?" his mom asked. "I'll pick you up in the morning."

"Can you drive me to the airport?"

"Yes," was the response.

"Great!" Mike said. "See you in the morning."

Mike hung up. "Is it okay for me to call my flight instructor?" Mike asked Alan.

"Sure."

"I need to tell her I made it," Mike said as he dialed. But there was no answer. "I'll call her tomorrow. I'm going to turn in. I'm beat and have a long trip back tomorrow."

"Have a good night," Alan said. "In case I'm gone by the time you get up, I hope your flight back goes smoother than your landing here."

"I'll say amen to that. But I'm not worried. God is with me."

The night seemed short. Too soon, Mike heard Lynne's voice through the bedroom door. "Someone on the phone for you," she said.

The morning sun was blinding. He got up. "I'll be right there."

"Hello," Mike mumbled, rubbing his eyes.

"This is Novato Airport. When we came to work this morning, we noticed your plane parked in the wrong place."

"Sorry about that. I didn't know where to park it last night. That's why I left my phone number in the mailbox."

"We appreciate it. When can you move it?"

"It's about nine now. Probably before 10 o'clock."

"Super. We'll see you soon."

Mike's mom knocked on the door. "Ready?" she said, as he let her in.

"Just about. I'll get my things. We need to stop by the airport."

"All right."

"Thanks for everything, Lynne. I slept good last night."

"Have a good flight back. It was good to see you, even for a short time." Lynne gave him a quick hug.

"Hope this doesn't take too much time," Mike worried as his mother steered the white Cadillac into the airport. "I want to get an early start so I'll have plenty of daylight. Don't want a repeat of last night."

"What time do you want to take off?" his mother asked.

"No later than one p.m."

"Here we are," his mother said, as they pulled up to the small terminal.

"I'll be only a few minutes," Mike said, as he shut the car door. "Wait here."

So that's what the hill looks like, Mike mused, heading toward his plane. *It looks like the hunched back of a giant camel.*

He moved the plane and returned to the terminal. *Think I'll call in my flight plan now,* he decided. *That will save time later.* The airport had a direct line to the Oakland Flight Service. He also checked the weather.

Now all I have to do when I come back is take off. Then call on the radio to open my flight plan.

Mike and his mom drove to Tiburon. His folks wanted him to have a good meal before he took off.

"You're eating too fast," Mike's dad noticed. "What's your hurry?"

"Dad, I'd feel a lot more comfortable if I could take off as soon as possible. I want to be back before dark. I want nothing like last night to happen again."

"Well, neither do we. Let's go." His father stood up in front of the large glass window overlooking the San Francisco Bay and city. "We have a couple of stops, but we'll get you there on time."

"A couple of stops?" Mike worried.

"It won't take long," Mike's dad assured him.

First, they stopped at a grocery store. That took 20 minutes. Their next stop was at a bank. While he and his mother waited in the car, Mike went over his chart.

Should I take the Central California route, or go back on the coast? Mike pondered. *Which way would be faster? Guess I'll stick with the coastal route. I've already got the chart made out for that.*

Finally they headed toward the airport. By the time they got there it was around two p.m.

"You know," Mike said, "it's close to the time that I got off yesterday."

"Sorry, son. I'll drive you right up to the plane."

"It's okay, Dad. At least if it gets dark by the time I get back to FlaBob, I know the area well. I wouldn't be a stranger there as I was here last night."

Maybe I should spend another night here, Mike thought. *That's not necessary,* he reasoned to himself. *I do know the area down there.*

"It's a good day for flying," Mike told his folks as they got out of the car.

Mike climbed aboard and turned the key. Nothing happened.

"The battery is dead," Mike called to his dad from the cockpit.

"What now?" his dad asked.

"I'll handprop it," Mike replied. He jumped out.

"Mike, have you done this before?"

"Sure," Mike answered. "Don't worry, Dad. Climb in the cockpit and push down on the brakes while I start this thing."

His dad climbed into the cockpit. Mike walked to the front of the plane.

"Clear!" Mike shouted. He pulled down on the propeller. The engine started right up.

Mike took his seat in the cockpit and taxied over to the fuel pumps, charging the battery on the way. By the time the attendant had topped off the tanks and Mike was ready to go, it was about 10 minutes after two.

"This is it," Mike said to his folks, as he signed the gas receipt.

"God be with you," his mother said. They embraced. Mike climbed back into the cockpit, started the engine, taxied, and took off. His folks waved from the ground.

As Mike climbed, he called Oakland Flight Service and opened his flight plan. It was 2:30 p.m.

This time Mike was not cheated out of his view of the bay as he had been the night before by darkness. It was breathtaking.

"2499 Juliet," a call crackled over his radio.

"That's me!" Mike realized.

"This is 2499 Juliet," Mike responded. "Go ahead."

"You filed a five-hour flight plan with only three hours of fuel aboard—but you did not file a fuel stop."

"My refueling stop will be at San Luis Obispo."

As Mike flew over the Golden Gate bridge, he saw a huge cargo ship sailing under the graceful span. The day was clean and clear. Banking south and heading down the coast, Mike set his receiver to a VOR frequency from his chart, using the same frequency he used coming up. It didn't work.

Oh no! It suddenly dawned on him. *These headings won't work!* All the frequency headings had to be refigured in the opposite direction from the previous day's flight. Having never plotted a there-and-back cross country trip before, but only round-robins—or circle routes—Mike had thought the course already plotted on the chart would work both ways.

How could I have thought that! he chastised himself.

But of course, he had not thought about it at all. He had never had occasion to.

Other flight instructors told Mike later that before signing a student pilot off for a cross-country solo, an instructor is required to check the student's charting for the entire trip. Elaine checked only the first leg of Mike's cross country but not his return leg. It is critical that a flight instructor check a student's charting for the entire route. Flight training is a learning experience, and if required steps are left out, a student may not be learning them.

I wish I could fly back to Novato! Mike worried. *Then I could refigure all of my VOR headings and start out earlier tomorrow morning. But Elaine needs the plane. If I kept it over another night she couldn't use it for her students. She would lose money.*

A plane's rental charge is based on time in the air, not on time spent sitting on the ground. Mike knew Elaine was operating on a shoestring budget. That was why her rates were going up over the weekend.

Better continue, Mike decided. He spread his chart out over the tiny cockpit to refigure the frequencies and compass headings. He was still climbing; he passed near Palo Alto.

He also had to refigure his time from each VOR station and how long it would take to reach San Luis Obispo for refueling. When he finished, he was nearing Half Moon Bay and flying over Santa Cruz.

I'll never make it to San Luis Obispo by 5 o'clock, when the pumps close, he realized. *I'll refuel at Monterey instead.* He slipped his plane between the hills and landed at the small airport.

Sure is getting late, Mike thought as the gas attendant fueled the tanks. *Almost five o'clock and I have more than three hours to go! I'll call Elaine to see if I can stay up here one more night.*

"Hey," Mike asked the attendant, "where's the pay phone?"

"Over there," the man answered, pointing to a small building about 100 yards away.

I hope she will tell me to stay up here. Mike half ran to the phone.

Where is her phone number? Mike fingered the papers in his wallet. *Here it is.*

His heart began to sink as Elaine's office phone rang on without answer.

I'll try her home phone. Mike dialed the new number.

"Hello," said a woman's voice.

"Elaine? This is Mike."

"No, it's Terry." Terry was Elaine's partner in the flight school. "Elaine is not here. May I help you?"

"Yes. I'm getting a late start back. I'm worried about time and thinking about staying up here another night."

Terry was silent.

"I know the plane is reserved tomorrow for another student. Right?"

"Yes," she replied. "We do need the plane."

"Okay, which way would save me more time, the coast or the inland route?"

"I don't know which way is fastest," answered Terry. "Use your own judgment."

"It's getting pretty late," Mike continued. "I'm not checked out for night flying yet."

"Use your own judgment," she repeated.

It's nearly five o'clock! Mike thought to himself. *From what I've told her, she thinks I'm still north of San Francisco. Yet she still seems to want me to fly down today! They must really need the plane tomorrow!*

"Okay, I'll fly down today and take the coastal route."

"Fine," she responded. "We'll see you tonight."

Once Mike decided to go ahead and finish the trip, the matter was settled. *I'm going home!* He walked back to the fuel pumps, signed the gas receipt, and climbed aboard the plane. He taxied down the runway and took off.

As he cleared the runway and began his climb, he glanced down to see Monterey nestled among the dark, twisted pine trees along the coast. Ocean waves washed against the shore. Rays of the late afternoon sun seemed to be reflected by millions of tiny mirrors floating on ocean swells.

The previous year, Ann Louise and Mike had driven through this same area on California Highway 1, the twisting route that snakes along the coast of California. They took their time and stopped frequently. They took many pictures of one another, with the ocean as a backdrop.

I wish she were here with me now and could see this, Mike thought as he banked his plane south along the coast.

Mike was still climbing when he tried to contact the Oakland Flight Service to let them know he had changed his fuel stop.

"Oakland Flight Service, this is 2499 Juliet. Do you copy?"

No answer—just static.

"Oakland Flight Service. Come in."

Again no response. He was too far out of range for them to pick up his call; he was also too inexperienced to realize that that was the problem and that he should try another flight service station. *At least I have plenty of fuel to make it home*, he thought.

CHAPTER

5

U se your own judgment."
Terry's words lingered in Mike's mind as he flew over
Carmel. As late as it was, his best judgment was to try to
make the best time possible so he would at least arrive in
familiar territory before dark. One way to save time was to
maintain maximum speed.

*I'll make a gradual ascent to 2,000 feet along the coast. Then
I'll bank inland at Morro Bay and continue climbing to around
5,500 feet.*

Climbing steeply all at once takes longer than climbing
gradually. Making a plane climb into the sky is much the
same as making a car climb a mountain. The steeper the
climb, the slower the car goes. Even stepping harder on
the gas pedal may not maintain the speed if the climb is
too steep. However, if the driver can choose to climb
gradually he can maintain maximum speed. That is what
Mike decided to do.

The sun was dropping lower in the sky on his right as
he flew down the coast. Again he saw those sandy coves
with cliffs towering over them.

As he looked at the Pacific Coast Highway bending
around those coves, he recognized some of the spots
where Ann Louise and he had stopped to look around on
their trip the previous year.

An hour and a half later, Mike turned inland and

switched his frequency to the Santa Barbara VOR. He was about 2,000 feet high.

Straight ahead of him, 50 miles away, rose the San Rafael Mountains. The day before, he had gone around these mountains. Today he planned to go over them, to save time. From the map it seemed simple.

The 15 to 20 minutes I'll save could mean the difference between dusk and darkness at the end of my trip, Mike thought. *The extra daylight time could put me well into the Los Angeles Basin, an area where I know the freeways and buildings as landmarks—even at night.*

The gentle-looking, rolling San Rafael Mountains are an anomaly among California mountains. In that state, most ranges lie north to south, more or less paralleling the coast. The San Rafaels run in an east-west line, separating the Los Angeles Basin from Santa Barbara.

The San Rafael Mountains are sliced by several main fault systems and thousands of smaller ones, some never even mapped. As water eroded the layers of ancient sandstone, canyons were carved along these faults. These canyons have wall-like sides, treacherous because of their crumbly nature.

The highest peak in the area, Big Pine Mountain, is a little under 7,000 feet high. But Mike was not going over that peak. His course would take him over a range considerably lower.

How much lower, Mike couldn't tell for sure. A problem with the WAC map was that, in its lack of detail, it did not give the elevation of that range. He could see it was lower, however. It looked as if it was less than 5,000 feet high.

The range is 30 minutes away, Mike calculated. *With my throttle wide open, and an airspeed of 110 mph, and climbing 250 feet per minute, I'll have plenty of altitude to make it over that range.*

Keeping his eye on the rate-of-climb gauge, he set the trim tab, a black wheel located between the seats. When adjusted by turning, pressure was applied on the back elevator located at the rear of the plane. This kept the plane in a nose-up attitude to maintain his 250 fpm climb.

Mike was heading in a southeasterly direction and flying through a wide valley between two mountain ranges. The late afternoon sun cast an orange-red glow over the valley, accentuating the canyons with deep shade. At the end of the valley he could see where the two ranges were joined together by another range, making a U. Mike planned to fly over the connecting range.

He glanced at the altimeter from time to time, much as a driver occasionally checks his speedometer. More often, he checked his rate-of-climb gauge, because that was the instrument that dictated continuing adjustments on the trim tab to keep it where he wanted it.

Not too much longer, he thought as he leaned back in his seat. *So far so good.*

But there were a number of things Mike did not know, since he was a student pilot with minimal flight experience and no ground schooling. For one thing, he did not know he was flying under a constant downdraft that acted like a giant hand holding him down. Flowing up and over the range was a steady stream of northerly winds blowing at 10 to 14 knots—the same March winds that had slowed him down the day before. Without ground school, where different types of wind conditions are taught, he was unaware of this kind of a downdraft. The rate-of-climb instrument on which he was depending may also have been malfunctioning.

As he approached the end of the horseshoe-shaped valley, he saw a pass that cut through the range, but his WAC didn't give its elevation. *I'll take that*, he decided. *It's lower. I won't need to gain as much altitude that way.*

Darkness was fast approaching. That worried him.

But as Mike flew toward the pass he could see only its beginning. He could not see where it broke through. Mike strained against his shoulder harness. He released it. *That's better. But where does the pass break through?*

Better go back. No sense taking chances. His speed was

more than 100 miles an hour.

Mike banked to the left to make his turn. But he was farther into the pass than he realized.

There's not enough room! he realized with horror as he saw that the arc of his turn would intersect a wall of rock. *I can't turn tight enough! I need more space!*

Twirling the yoke the other way, he pointed the plane back toward the pass.

But now it was too late for that too.

He was trapped in a dead-end canyon with towering rock walls all around him.

Beads of sweat broke out on his face like a rash.

There's no way out! His flesh sizzled. The canyon was too narrow to turn around in and too high to fly over.

I'm a dead man! Mike felt cold, like a lump of lifeless meat.

No! He refused to give up. He banked to the left as far as he could, then whipped back to the right.

I've got to get over the wall before it gets any steeper!

His throttle was wide open. The engine screamed. His arms gripped the wheel like steel. He was headed toward a wall of rock!

The stall-warning buzzer shrieked.

My air speed! It's dropping! I'm going to stall!

The wall of rock rushed toward him.

Mike didn't know he was bucking winds spilling over the range. He didn't know that at 5,000 feet the air was too thin for a small plane like a Cessna 150 to gain enough power to make that kind of a climb.

It seemed that the hot winds of hell burst over him. He couldn't breathe. His cockpit was a sealed glass jar and he had used up all the air.

Time stood still.

A deeper, much deeper struggle filled his soul. It was not a struggle for life. He knew he was a dead man. But he saw in his life very little that was good.

I'm not worthy of heaven, he anguished, even though he knew God does not save man because of his goodness.

As a Christian, Mike never imagined he would be afraid to face death. He knew that death is but a sleep and when he awoke he would see his Saviour's second coming.

But I don't want to die!

Mike wanted to pray but didn't have time. He said it all in a single name.

"Jesus!"

He remembers nothing else. His plane smashed into the wall of rock.

6

Except for the gentle rustle of the wind, all was silent.

Mike's eyes fluttered open. He was slumped over in his seat. With great effort he lifted his head and tried to look around, but darkness dimmed his vision. The sun was setting beyond the ridges, and dark mountain shadows were all about.

The plane had crashed into a canyon wall at an elevation of about 5,000 feet. But instead of tumbling to the canyon floor, a fall of about 600 feet, the plane perched like a huge dragonfly on a tiny shelf sticking out from the wall. Chaparral bushes lined the juncture where the shelf met the canyon wall. They had softened the plane's impact.

Mike was groggy. He looked at the chaparral leaves hungrily. The thought crossed his mind to eat them. It was unreal. He had no memory of anything, not even whether he was man or beast.

He gazed into the rear view mirror and saw an unfamiliar face, dark with dried blood. The left eyelid was still dripping, fresh blood coagulating on top of dried blood like candle wax. Fresh blood erupted through the crust on other parts of his face. No flesh was visible.

What is that? he wondered.

Moments passed in confusion.

Who am I? How did I get here?

He looked around some more.

Looks like a crashed airplane, Mike thought, uncomprehendingly.

I must be dreaming.

He tried to wake up, but couldn't.

If I'm not dreaming, what am I doing in a crashed plane?

It was hard to think straight. It was like waking up in the middle of the night on vacation in a strange hotel, only worse.

He did his best to concentrate.

Finally he remembered who he was. Then he remembered his trip to San Francisco.

Oh, that's right! I was flying back from my folks!

Then everything came back to him. He remembered facing the wall of rock and how he thought he was dead before he hit the side of the canyon wall.

Suddenly a well of joy sprang up inside him. He looked into the mirror on the panel again. This time he saw a row of white teeth in the blood-darkened face. He was smiling.

"I'm alive!" he exclaimed. "Praise God! I'm going to make it!"

Suddenly he was aware of incredible pain. It jabbed through his chest and arms like a sword. His upper left arm and shoulder had been shattered like a jigsaw puzzle when he slammed against the door on impact. Both lower forearms were also broken.

Mike groaned as he looked at his twisted left arm and winced as he repositioned it on his lap.

On the floor of the plane he saw his watch ticking towards seven o'clock. The band had been torn apart in the crash. It looked as though some crazed rat had chewed on it. He had been unconscious perhaps an hour, with maybe five minutes spent trying to make sense out of things, getting his memory back.

Mike looked around slowly in the dim light. The canyon walls dropped away on both sides of the plane.

The wings and tail of the plane hung out over the tiny shelf. Through the rear window he could see that he was pretty far up from the floor of the canyon.

The air cooled as it got dark. The winds started flowing upward from the canyon. The plane rocked back and forth, making a crunching sound like an old wooden ship.

Hope this baby stays up here, Mike worried. *If she slides off, I'll be a·goner for sure.*

The door on his side was jammed open. On the steep grade outside, he could see his suitcase and other belongings that had been thrown out on impact. One of the things he noticed beside the plane was the steering wheel.

How did that thing get out there? he wondered.

He remembered how a friend's brother had been killed in a plane crash when the steering wheel went through his chest and neck on impact. But in Mike's case the whole steering wheel with the column attached to it evidently had made a clean break and exited the cockpit before Mike slammed into the dashboard.

Mike shivered. *Where is my jacket?* He looked around. It lay outside the open door, a teasingly short distance from him. *Wonder if I could reach it.*

As the sun's rays disappeared, the temperature plunged. Even though it was nearly spring, snowfields still hung on northern slopes. *The terrain looks steep and rough,* Mike thought. *I'd better wait till morning so I can see what's going on.*

The radio! Mike exclaimed to himself. *I wonder if I can get it to work. Sure would like to help them find me faster.*

Nothing. Mike fiddled with the dials. *It's dead! I wish I could let Ann Louise know that I'm alive.*

Then he remembered the emergency locator transmitter (ELT) that all planes are required to carry. It is a little box with a long antenna that sends off a directional signal when it gets a heavy jolt. It is usually mounted in the tail section of the aircraft, but this one had been mounted in the baggage compartment right behind Mike's seat. He could not see it at all. *I hope it is working.*

Then he was thunderstruck by a horrible realization: *I crashed south of San Luis Obispo!* He hadn't reached the Oakland Flight Service to let them know he changed his fuel stop. That meant that when the searchers started looking for him, they'd check first with San Luis Obispo to see if he'd made it that far. When they found out he hadn't stopped there, they'd think he crashed north of there.

It might take them longer to find me, Mike thought, *but I'll be found. The Lord is with me.*

By this time Mike could not see anything in the darkness. He decided to lie down. He swung himself around and dangled his lower legs out the open door on the pilot's side. With the slightest movement, pain flashed through his body like lightning.

Mike tried to prop his head against the opposite door, but every maneuver sent waves of pain hurtling through his body.

This is probably the best I can do, he thought as he lay across the seats. The icy winds compounded his misery. He had not much to shield him from the cold—only his turtle-necked sweater and jeans. The sweater helped some, but still he shivered. He had no food or water. He tucked his useless left arm under his belt to keep it stable.

"Lord," Mike prayed, "be with those who are looking for me. Help them to find me soon. I don't know how long I can survive up here."

Mike called," Linda said when Ann Louise returned from lunch. "He will be landing at FlaBob around 6:30 tonight. He said he'd call when he arrives. Then you can pick him up."

"Thanks," Ann Louise replied. She walked into her office.

I have only a few things to do, Ann Louise thought, looking at the paperwork on her desk. *I'll get done what I can now, do some shopping, and then go home to wait for Mike's call.*

Ann Louise got home just before 6:30 and puttered around, expecting to hear the phone ring at any moment. About the time Mike was wishing that he could let her know that he was alive, she began to worry about not receiving his call.

It is getting pretty close to eight o'clock, Ann Louise worried. *I should have heard from him by now.*

I'll check with Elaine, she thought. She flipped through the phone book but could not remember the instructor's last name. *Maybe the airport has her home number.* But as she looked through the phone book she remembered that Mike said to call the Ontario Flight Service for information about his flight. They keep track of flight plans that pilots file.

"Your husband should be landing any moment, Mrs.

Chambers," said someone at the flight service.

"Thank you, I'll wait for his call."

But there was no phone call.

An awful feeling started growing inside her with each passing minute. She tried to busy herself with other things, but it did not stop the panic slowly engulfing her. Mike knew how much she worried and was always very careful to reassure her of his safety.

"Dear Lord," Ann Louise prayed, "be with him."

The minutes ticked slowly to nine o'clock and still no call. Again she called the flight service.

"Hello," she said anxiously. "This is Ann Louise Chambers and my husband Mike hasn't called."

"Mrs. Chambers, we have started a communications check of the airports along his proposed flight path to see if he made an unscheduled landing."

"Why would he do that?" she asked.

"Pilots have been known to land at airports along their routes to visit friends or relatives without letting us know about it."

"Mike wouldn't stop without notifying anyone," she said.

"We do a communications check first. If it turns out negative, an air search is started. I assure you, Mrs. Chambers, we will contact you as soon as we learn anything."

Discovering they had already started a search unnerved Ann Louise further. She went over and over in her mind any eventuality other than a crash. *Could he have possibly stopped over anywhere? Would he stop at Santa Barbara at his sister's? No.* She forced herself to wait until 10 o'clock before calling again, but it was merely a repeat of her nine o'clock call.

To take her mind away from her building panic, she decided to read, and pulled out a volume of Sherlock Holmes short stories. *Something devotional or religious would probably be more appropriate,* she thought. *But that wouldn't divert my thoughts.*

Fear engulfed her like a thick cloud. She started to cry. She would read a tale, cry, read another, and cry some more. She doubts that she will ever again be able to read Sherlock Holmes with pleasure.

Missy and Dumpling, their two cats, unlike the reputation of their breed, have always been affectionate and responsive, coming to her call. Now they curled up beside her on the couch, as if to provide comfort.

Ann Louise's mind kept going in circles. *What could be happening to Mike? Something is wrong. He might be dead. If he's not dead, whatever has happened, he needs help. Where could he be?*

She felt so helpless and lost at not knowing. Just weeks before, a plane that had crashed 17 years earlier had finally been discovered in the mountains near their home.

When no call had come by 11 o'clock, her mind had fully exhausted any possibilities other than a crash. Again she called the flight service.

"Ontario Flight Service," someone answered.

She clenched her fists and breathed deeply for a moment in order to talk without breaking down. But as soon as she spoke, her composure dissolved.

"This is Ann Louise Chambers," she sobbed. "Could anything have happened other than a crash?"

"Oh, yes," the attendant said encouragingly. "Sometimes a pilot hears something strange in the engine and decides to set down at a small airstrip to check it out. If the airstrip is closed, he might not be able to get to a phone to let anyone know he is there. Or there might not be an airstrip and the pilot may decide to land in a field. That would make getting to a phone even harder, but, of course, could still mean he might be all right."

It didn't sound very reassuring.

"How long would a plane float," she asked, "if it ditched in the ocean?"

"It depends on whether or not the gas tanks were full," he answered. "If the tanks were nearly empty, a plane would float longer than if the tanks had just been filled."

"What about the emergency locator transmitter? Would that give a signal under water? And how long might an oil slick last?"

"A signal couldn't be as strong under water. And how long an oil slick remains would depend on the amount of fuel spilled and the condition of the sea."

Later she learned that his answers were somewhat misleading, even if well-intentioned. According to Air Force personnel she talked to, a Cessna 150 has the flotation properties of a brick. And with the exception of highly skilled and experienced pilots, a pilot almost invariably is stunned by the impact of the landing gear hitting the water and goes down with the plane in seconds.

I'll call Mike's folks, she decided. But, being so upset, she could not find the number that Mike had given her the afternoon before. She called Mike's brother Alan.

"Hello," Lynne answered.

Ann Louise could not talk. She tried, but only garbled words came out.

"Who is this?" Lynne asked. "Ann Louise, is that you? What's the matter?"

Ann Louise finally got out that Mike had not arrived and that she could not find his parents' number.

"Is anyone with you?" Lynne asked.

"No," she sobbed.

"Call someone to stay with you, Ann Louise. I'll call Mike's dad."

Ann Louise hung up.

It's late, Ann Louise thought. *What could anyone do?*

She did not realize what a comfort it would be to have someone with her.

After her 11 o'clock call she started receiving calls from the rescue station at McClellan Air Force Base, the center that coordinated the initial search efforts. They asked her many questions.

"What was his experience?" they asked.

"Nearly 40 hours of flying," she answered.

"Would he be likely to make any side trips?"

"No."

"Was there anyone he might have stopped to visit?"

"No."

"Might he have had anything alcoholic to drink before taking off?"

"No, he doesn't drink."

"Do you know anything that might give us a clue as to where to look?"

"No."

These questions she answered over and over again. At each new shift change, they called her back to ask the same questions. She learned later from the Civil Air Patrol manual that a victim's family should be questioned only once and the information passed on to units and shifts needing it. But even though she had to answer the same questions over and over, she did not mind. It reassured her that someone was doing something.

"Ann Louise." Mike's dad was on the phone. "What's happening?"

Ann Louise filled him in on all she knew.

"He is not a daredevil," Mike's dad said. "He's very cautious about his flying."

Whatever might have happened, they knew Mike would have been using his best judgment. They remembered how carefully Mike followed regulations as he knew them. When he bucked head winds on the flight up, he had radioed to the flight service to extend his flight plan.

Soon after Mike's dad hung up, the flight service called again. "The communication check turned up negative. Tomorrow we will start a physical search."

"But if he's down, he needs help now!" Ann Louise said.

"It's dark," was the reply. "We'll start at sunrise."

It's best not to crash after office hours. An air search cannot start until every airstrip along the flight path verifies by a physical check that the plane in question is not there. Once a field is closed, it is difficult to rouse anyone to go out and make the verification.

Knowing sleep would be difficult, Ann Louise settled herself on the living room hide-a-bed so that she would be close to the downstairs phone should it ring during the night. Mike had disconnected the ring mechanism on the upstairs phone so that he could sleep undisturbed after his night shifts.

Ann Louise prayed and dozed off around two o'clock Friday morning.

8

After the Ontario FAA Flight Service spoke to Ann Louise, they contacted the Western Rescue Center, the 42nd Air Rescue Squadron of the Military Airlift Command at McClellan Air Force Base.

"We have a possible downed plane."

"OK," the officer said. He put down his cup of coffee. "Give me a second to get a pen. Go ahead."

"This is what we have so far. Mike Chambers filed a flight plan with Oakland. He opened it about 2:30 this afternoon. His expected arrival time was 7:30 this evening at FlaBob Airport in Riverside. However, it's now 11:30 and so far he hasn't closed it. About an hour after Chamber's scheduled landing time, we talked to his wife. She hasn't heard anything from him either."

"Anything from the communications check?"

"Negative. We checked every airport on his flight path."

"What about his refueling stop?"

"Negative on that too. San Luis Obispo was his refueling point, but they told us Chambers didn't land there. If he did go down, it must have been north of San Luis Obispo."

"Our work is cut out for us tonight. What else do you have?"

"Chambers reported that his plane is a Cessna 150, high wing, red and white."

"Got it. With no word from Chambers and a negative communications check, it doesn't look good. We'll take it from here."

When the Western Rescue Center had digested the information of Mike's flight, they called the Civil Air Patrol (CAP).

The CAP was founded in World War II as a branch of the United States Air Force. During the war the Air Force was so involved overseas that they needed help on the home front for patrol. So a group of light airplane pilots volunteered their time and resources to patrol the American coastlines for enemy submarines. Off the coast of California some of them even carried small bombs strapped under their planes.

After the war was over they became a volunteer search and rescue operation for downed aircraft. Today the Civil Air Patrol is composed of dedicated men and women who are involved in saving the lives of downed pilots. The moment they get word that an aircraft is missing, they drop everything, including work, and immediately start the procedure of looking for the downed pilot. They are not paid for this service.

"The phone is ringing." Bruce's wife shook him gently.

"What time is it?" Bruce reached for the light switch.

"Around 1:30 a.m.," Thelma answered.

It was early Friday morning when Captain Bruce Gordon, CAP mission control officer for the State of California, got the first call from McClellan. A mission control officer gathers all the data about a downed plane and coordinates the rescue operation.

"Hello," said Bruce sitting up in bed in his Santa Barbara home.

"We have a missing aircraft."

"OK," Bruce said, instantly awake. "Fill me in and I'll get started."

The rescue center gave him the flight details. Bruce, an experienced flyer himself, jotted the information down on a pad he kept on his nightstand for just this purpose.

After receiving the flight data, he notified Betty Meola, of San Jose, California, the mission coordinator.

"Good morning, Betty," Bruce said, in his Andy Griffin way.

"Good morning to you, Bruce, if you can call it that," Betty said half awake. "For you to call me in the middle of the night, we must have a missing plane."

"Unfortunately, yes," Bruce responded.

Bruce filled her in and Betty went to work. Later she would go to the San Jose airport to set up a search base to coordinate the search. But first she would call the squadron leaders from home. She dialed the first number.

"Joe, this is Betty. We have a possible downed pilot."

"Roger. I'll notify my pilots to get ready for a morning air search. What about the other squadron leaders?"

"I'll call them too," Betty answered. "The search area is large and involves other sectors."

"We'll be ready at dawn."

At daybreak Bruce Gordon called Major Burnham, the CAP information officer. His job was twofold: first, to receive civilian information about Mike's flight, such as if someone had spotted a low-flying plane or heard the noise of a crash. He also handles the press. When a plane goes down, the media wants to know all about it. They contact him.

Bruce also called the state Office of Emergency Services (OES). Their job is to notify all the state law agencies that a rescue operation is underway. OES then called the California Highway Patrol, the sheriff's departments, and the forest rangers.

"I'm going to recheck the airports along Mike's flight route," Bruce told Thelma.

"Didn't the FAA already check them?" she asked.

"Yes, but it's eight o'clock and daylight now. Even the

small airports should be open. I'll double-check just in case they missed anything."

While Bruce was making these calls, Betty had airplanes in the air, flying Mike's flight route from Novato south to San Luis Obispo.

Bruce stayed by the phone, hoping and praying to hear that Mike would be found alive.

CHAPTER
9

Mike tried to sleep, but pain flashed through his body with each movement. He dozed fitfully. Seconds dragged on like minutes, minutes like hours. The early light of dawn was a relief.

As the sun's first rays illuminated the blood-spattered cockpit, Mike looked around. *What a night! I've had better.* Still lying across the seats, he moved gingerly, then dragged himself up to a sitting position. He groaned with pain. *I wonder how long will it take them to find me?*

Where is my jacket? Shivering, he remembered that it was outside the cockpit on the steep rocks. *I must get it.*

But the slightest movement sent pain slicing through his body, like a butcher slicing a piece of meat with a razor-sharp knife.

Why is there so much pain? Mike wondered. *It feels like more than my arms are broken. I hurt all over!*

Mike looked through the broken-out windshield of the craft. The canyon walls loomed around him. He tried the radio again. Nothing. *I wonder what's wrong.* Mike examined the rest of the panel. *The instruments look okay. The radio should work.* He looked through the broken windshield again.

Aha. The engine is ripped off its mounts.

Maybe the battery cables are disconnected. There is no power! Now Mike knew what he needed to do.

I've got to get out there. I'll hook up the battery and get the radio working. I can also get my jacket.

That was easier said than done. As he prepared himself to leave the cockpit, the pain intensified. He blacked out momentarily.

I might not be able to get back into the cockpit once I get out, he realized. He took the radio mike and hung it out the passenger window, the side where the battery was, and turned the dial to the emergency frequency. *That way I can work the radio from outside the cockpit,* he figured.

He worked himself toward the jammed-open door slowly, agonizing with every movement. He paused on the ledge of the doorway. Only the main body of the plane was on the rock shelf. The wings and tail hung out over space.

Boy, that's steep. Mike shivered. *If I had crashed ten feet in any direction I would have hit sheer rock.* He pictured his plane bursting into flames and tumbling hundreds of feet down to the floor of the canyon in a ball of fire.

Well, it's not going to get any better. Guess this is it. Mike pushed himself out of the craft and dropped about two feet to the ground. Groaning, he rolled over his jacket. *I'll get it in a minute,* he thought, waiting for the pain to subside.

But Mike's problems were just beginning. As he tried to stand up, violent pain shot through his whole body. He screamed and collapsed on the rocks, writhing.

Something else must be broken! he anguished. *Maybe my hip.* He didn't even consider a broken back. He thought broken backs meant paralysis. But in reality his back was broken in three places. *My jacket!* he remembered. But he had rolled past it. Horrified, he stretched out his hand. He could not reach it.

The cold piercing winds pricked his flesh like needles.

Mike could not get his jacket. He could not fix the radio. He could not walk. He was cold, hurting, and helpless.

"Lord," he prayed, "help them to find me."

Now another problem became evident and it was ominous: he was sliding. Small stones like tiny ball bearings covered the steep slope. With each breath Mike slid a few inches, sometimes more. At times he thought he had stopped sliding, but he hadn't. He slid inch by slow inch. At least the sun was beginning to warm the rocks.

But suddenly he was alert to his danger. *A cliff!*

His breathing betrayed him. It seemed to steal away his life by inches. With each breath, stones trickled out from under him, like waves stealing sand from under one's feet on the seashore. He rolled onto his stomach as he approached the edge of the ledge. It looked like a seven to ten foot drop. *I could land on my head.* He positioned himself so that he would go off feet first. *That way the fall won't be such a long drop.*

He slid off the cliff, landing feet first. He tumbled onto his side and rolled onto his back. Intense pain radiated through his body.

I don't think anything else broke, Mike thought, continuing to slide.

He looked up. He was under the shelf that supported the plane. He could see the tail section hanging over the ledge.

Hope it doesn't break loose and fall on me. He shoved himself so that his sliding would take him away from the potential path of the plane, should it give way.

But the plane was more secure than Mike was. The surface that Mike had fallen to was the same kind that he had left—hard rock covered with tiny ball-bearing-like stones. And with each breath he kept on sliding.

The sun's rays continued to warm the air. Seemingly no longer moving, Mike's mind drifted to scenes of walking on Laguna's beaches with Ann Louise, a favorite outing of theirs, and then browsing in beach shops, looking at the paintings and pottery made by local artists and artisans. And then lunch at a sidewalk cafe, enjoying the salty ocean breeze.

As Mike thought of Ann Louise, a different pain

welled up inside him, not the physical pain from his injuries but the agony of realizing what she must be going through. *I wish I could let her know I'm alive.*

From his new vantage point he could see the layout of the canyon a lot better. The rugged walls looked as if they'd been chiseled out by some giant hand. Sections of the canyon wall dropped straight down, 600 feet to the bottom. Sloping sections, like that he was on, gathered debris, small rocks and dirt. Other parts of this canyon had deep crevasses where bushes grew. Mike could see the bottom of the canyon, and a valley that was lower than the canyon itself. Across the valley, a range of mountains loomed.

A sudden slippage of several feet yanked him back to reality. *I'm still sliding!* he realized, fear striking him like a lightning bolt.

Another cliff! His heart raced.

The second cliff was much bigger than the first. It protruded out, then cut back in sharply, with a sheer drop of 35 or 40 feet. That's as high as a four- or five-story building.

Mike rolled onto his stomach and dug the fingers of his right hand into the hard shale. They could get no hold. His left arm was useless. He pressed the side of his head into the earth and flattened his body against the steep slope as much as he could, but still he slid. Dirt and stones filled his mouth as he moved toward certain death.

His legs went over the edge. He dug his fingers harder into the dirt. His upper legs and waist went over. Then his complete left side. He felt his right hand pass over a small bush as he slid over the edge. He grabbed it. It stopped him momentarily. But he was dangling over the edge in thin air. And hanging on with a broken arm.

Mike tried to swing back up. No use. He peered over his right shoulder. *I can't see bottom!* He couldn't believe this was happening to him. He looked again and saw the bottom of the canyon, but it was so far down, a cluster of huge boulders and rocks.

"Lord," he prayed, "I don't understand. You helped me through the plane crash. But what about this cliff?"

I could use a dramatic rescue, he thought.

He couldn't hang on forever. In horror he felt his fingers begin to slip and his grip give way. He closed his eyes. He couldn't bear to watch himself splatter the boulders below like a ripe melon. He plunged through the air, feeling it rush by him. But something interfered with his dive. He smashed into something, not the bottom, but a jagged rock protruding from the face of the cliff. His right side slammed against it and broke a rib. It knocked the air out of him, like a prize fighter thrown a right punch to the stomach. His lower jaw smacked the rock as he raced by, cracking several teeth. Again he dropped through empty air. He landed on another ledge, feet first.

His right leg and ankle snapped. He fell over onto his left side. The ankle swelled rapidly. It felt like it was in a vise, with a sadistic giant turning the screw. *Got to get the boot off.* He bent over and unfastened it. His other boot was already off. He saw it on the ground a few feet away from him. *At least I'm alive*, he thought, surprise surfacing through the throbbing pulse of pain in his ankle and leg.

But the ground Mike had landed on was still covered with the small ball-bearing-like stones, and he was sliding again. As before, at times Mike thought he had stopped moving, but like the hour hand of a clock, although it's movement may not be perceived, it does move—and so did Mike.

He neared a third cliff. Because it was rounded and had no lip, Mike could not tell how much of a drop it would be. Fortunately, he fell only a few feet this time, but he landed on the same ankle that he had broken when he fell off the second cliff. Now the foot was totally twisted around and pointing behind him.

"Help me, Lord."

Still he slid. Breath by breath. Toward a fourth cliff. Like the second, this was a sheer drop, but this time it would be a drop of 300 feet, to the bottom of the canyon floor.

He saw a tree near the path of his descent. *I must get over to it*, he told himself. *It's my only chance.*

Lying on his back, Mike maneuvered himself so that his slide was in line with the tree. It worked. He slid down to it and caught the trunk of the tree at his waist. *At least I'm not going any further*, he realized with relief.

The sun was setting now. Mike had slid and fallen more than 300 feet. Twenty feet from him was the final cliff, with its 300-foot sheer drop to rocks and boulders.

Mike was punchy. A crazy thought entered his head. *I wonder if I still have my wallet.* He reached behind him to check. Instead of his back pocket he felt only bare flesh. The seat of his jeans was gone, torn and worn away by the sliding. When he pulled his hand back, he found it covered with blood. His exposed backside was bleeding. Stones were embedded in his hips and thighs. His sweater was rolled up under his arms, leaving his torso bare. He was too weak to pull it back down. Blood flowed from scrapes and cuts all over his body.

The warmth of the sun forsook him as it slipped below the mountains. Icy winds returned, even colder than the night before.

An ominous thought flickered in his mind, *You won't last the night.*

O K, thanks for checking."
Bruce placed the receiver back in the cradle and sat with his chin propped in his hands.

He turned to his wife. "That was the last of them—San Luis Obispo. I've checked all the airports down to Chamber's refueling stop. All negative."

"Anything from Betty yet?"

"No. Even the coast guard has been alerted and nothing from them either." Bruce looked at his charts.

"I wonder if Mike could have refueled earlier than he'd planned to." He studied the charts carefully. "Possibly at Monterey."

"Why there?" Thelma asked as Bruce picked up the phone.

"It's the closest airport north of San Luis Obispo's," he answered, dialing.

"Monterey Airport."

"Bruce Gordon again from the Civil Air Patrol."

"We already checked for Chamber's plane and didn't see it."

"I know, but could you check your gas receipts and look for his signature?"

"Sure. Be right back." The gas attendant crossed the room to a metal box in the corner. He removed a handful of slips and flipped through them as he returned to the phone.

"We're in luck," he said. "Chambers did refuel here yesterday."

"Thank you very much!" Bruce exclaimed. He dialed Betty at the search base. "Mike refueled at Monterey, not San Luis Obispo. He could have made it farther than San Luis Obispo. Contact your squadron leaders to extend the search south of there."

"I'll get right on it."

Bruce looked at his watch—4 p.m. already.

The phone rang. "This is Santa Barbara County Sheriff's substation. We just received a call from a pilot reporting a faint emergency radio signal."

"Where?" Bruce perked up.

"South of San Luis Obispo, near Big Pine Mountain."

"Thank you! Let me know if any more calls like that come in."

Bruce dialed the Santa Barbara Airport. "We're looking for a downed plane and just got a report of an ELT signal around Big Pine Mountain. Could you alert commercial traffic in that area to monitor the emergency frequency?"

"Will do," the controller responded.

"Thanks," Bruce said, already looking down at Betty's phone number for his next call.

"Betty, we've got a distress signal south of Obispo. We need one of our planes up there right away."

"I'll get someone from Santa Barbara."

"Good," Bruce said. "It could be Mike."

But by the time the Santa Barbara pilot was ready for takeoff, thick fog had rolled in and grounded all planes.

Betty called Fresno to locate a pilot there.

"You won't be able to see much," Betty told the pilot, Leland Stoudt, "but there's a signal to try to locate." Leland and his spotter took off. By the time they reached the area of the reported distress signal, it was shortly before midnight Friday night.

"Betty was right. Can't see much up here," Leland commented.

"Well, maybe we'll hear something," the observer said. They flew the grid pattern patiently, back and forth, back and forth. Then they carefully crisscrossed the area. It took hours. But they heard no distress signal.

"Doesn't sound like anyone is out there," Leland finally remarked. "Let's give it one more pass and call it a night."

Suddenly a weak signal sounded on the radio. "Bleep!"

"Did you hear that?" the observer said.

"Sure did," Leland answered. "Let's do another pass."

They heard the bleep again.

"That's it! We've found it!"

They radioed their coordinates back to Betty at the CAP search base station in San Jose.

"Wonder why the signal is so weak," the spotter commented.

The ELT had catapulted through Mike's windshield on impact. It broke half the windshield out, ricocheted off a large boulder in front of the plane, and then lodged under the left wing.

More critically, the signal was coming out of a narrow canyon. The signal pattern was a strip only six miles long and two miles wide. It reached up only a few hundred feet, not nearly high enough to be picked up by commercial traffic. Under better conditions, an ELT can give off a signal with a 50-mile radius.

"Guess that's all we can do now," Leland said. He seemed reluctant to leave.

"How about turning on our landing lights as a signal?" the spotter suggested. "If there is a survivor down there, it could encourage him."

"Good idea!" Leland responded. "Let's do it!" He made one more pass with their lights on, then flew away into the blackness of the night. But Mike did not see the landing lights.

"This is 5677 Dan calling search base," Leland radioed Betty as they flew back to Fresno. "We're on our way home, but we'll fly back at dawn to do a visual sighting."

"Roger," Betty said. "But contact Salinas in the morning instead of San Jose. Jerry Bollinger is taking over."

Betty called Bruce, "The spotter plane picked up the distress signal in your own backyard."

"Where?" Bruce asked looking at his map.

"South side of Big Pine Mountain, in the Los Padres Wilderness."

"Just where the other pilot reported it. I see it on the map in front of me."

It was three o'clock Saturday morning. Bruce sat at his desk alone.

If Mike is up there, we should be up there when the spotter plane returns. That way a ground crew can get to him as soon as possible.

Bruce started calling.

"Tired of sitting by your radio?" Bruce asked Major Lou Dartanner, the radio operator for the Santa Barbara CAP.

"It's been a long night," she said. "What do you have in mind?"

"Let's get our four-by-fours out there and try to get as close as possible to where the signal has been reported."

"Good idea," Lou said. "I'll call Joe Byrd and Ed Delauriers. We'll meet at your house."

"We'd better contact the forest rangers also to open up the gates along the fire roads," Bruce suggested.

"Right," she said. "I'll call the Los Priestos station. Wally Acton and Elmer Barabere are on duty there. I'll tell them we're on our way."

Wally and Elmer saw the lights of the four-by-fours flash into the ranger's station. Leaving their cups of coffee behind, they jumped into their jeep to lead the way.

As the three vehicles snaked along the dirt road through the rugged Los Padres Wilderness, they came across one locked gate after another. Each time Wally jumped out to open it so they could proceed.

The route was treacherous. Rock walls towered on one side. Cliffs dropped away on the other; they climbed higher and higher into the wilderness in the predawn darkness.

"I'll see if I can pick up Mike's ELT signals," Bruce said. He rotated the dials on his portable direction finder, the Little L-PER, which he had invented.

"Bleep!" They all heard it.

"We're getting close!" exclaimed Bruce. "Maybe three to five miles away!"

At daybreak, the search plane from Fresno returned.

"I see the plane!" Leland radioed Salinas. "Contact the ground units. I'll circle the wreckage until they can identify."

"Roger," Jerry responded from the search base station.

"Bruce, the search plane is circling the wreckage. Try to identify."

"Roger."

"I think I see the search plane," Bruce said to Lou. He pointed across the valley to the mountain range on the other side. "Let's stop here."

Climbing out of their jeeps, they pointed their binoculars at the search plane, then scanned the terrain below.

Lou was the first to spot the downed plane. "There it is! On that patch of bare rock!"

Then the others spotted it. "It looks like a fly clinging to that cliff!"

Bruce set up a 60-power telescope to get a better look at the wreckage. The plane's numbers on the fuselage were clearly visible.

"2499J! It's the missing plane all right."

Bruce radioed Jerry at the Salinas search base. "The plane is intact with very little damage visible; the windshield does not even appear broken. There could be a survivor."

It was 7:25 a.m.

"Jerry, we need a chopper out here."

"Roger, Bruce. I'll contact Vandenberg Air Force Base." He signalled the base. "We need a helicopter to pick up a downed pilot."

"I'll get a crew together," replied Major Tony Dowd from Detachment 8 command. "Where do you need us?"

Jerry gave the coordinates. Dowd needed four men to make up the helicopter crew. He awakened Lieutenants Rick McCourt (aircraft commander) and Pat Miles, who were roommates in the officers' barracks. In minutes they reported to squadron operations on the flight line.

"Where do we make the pick up?" McCourt asked as he and Dowd walked out onto the heliport.

Dowd opened up the map and pointed. "Here is where the CAP found him."

As the two men approached the hangar that housed the Huey helicopter, they could see Senior Master Sergeant Paul McGehee, a maintenance superintendent, and Technical Sergeant Ron House, line chief, hauling the chopper out of the hangar, with the help of some others from base transient alert.

"Beaver 32" and its crew, Dowd, McCourt, Miles, and House, left Vandenberg as soon as the morning ground fog lifted.

Back in the mountains, the search party bounced on in their jeeps to Bluff Camp, an unmanned fire station. The other jeeps stopped behind Bruce. "I think this is as close as we're going to get by road," Bruce said. He set up his telescope again.

"Can you see it from here?" Lou asked. The others climbed out of their four-by-fours.

"Yeah, there she is," Bruce said. "It's sitting pretty high on the canyon wall."

"How far do you think it is?" one asked.

"Three miles or so from here," Bruce answered. "Who wants to go?"

Ed, Joe, and Wally, the forest ranger, volunteered.

"Here's a radio." Bruce handed Wally a transceiver. "We'll keep in contact with you. Looks like you can follow this trail a little way down through this valley, but sooner or later you'll probably have to make your own trail through some pretty heavy brush."

"We'll make it," Wally said.

Shortly before eight a.m., Ed, Joe, and forest ranger Wally began hiking toward the plane. The trail was muddy and slippery, with patches of snow on it. The first mile was relatively easy, but then they had to leave the trail. They climbed over rocks and crawled under tangled and twisted brush. Much of the way they went on their bellies, squirming and straining for every foot.

"You know something?" Wally remarked.

"What?" Sweat dripped from their faces.

"I'm a three-year veteran in this back country. But I've never had a hike as hard as this one."

It took them nearly two hours of exhausting struggle just to get close to the crash site. They were tired.

"Where's the plane?"

Wally pointed to a spot hundreds of feet above them up in the dead-end canyon.

"Looks like our work has just started," another said, breathing heavily. He collapsed on a rock.

"We'll rest here a few minutes," Wally said, "then tackle the canyon wall."

Little did they know the risk that lay ahead of them.

11

As the night wore on, a different feeling washed over Mike. He could feel his life force flowing out, like water from a broken vase. A sense of desolation came upon him. Even his pain seemed to vanish. He felt only thirst.

The night got colder and darker. A coyote howl broke the silence. Through the empty canyon the howl echoed to the mountains afar. The howl portended Mike's death song, the cold night his coffin, and the canyon his grave.

But Mike was not yet ready to be buried. Like a candle whose flame is gone, leaving only a glow in the wick, Mike hung on.

"Lord," he prayed, "I want to see Ann Louise again." Dreamlike pictures of her passed through his mind. He saw her face, her smile.

His breathing became shallow. He could not move. He felt as if his body functions were shutting down like the machinery on a giant plane as the pilot throws the switches at the end of a long trip.

"Lord, don't forsake me," Mike whispered faintly. The cold arms of death wrapped around him. "Everything is a blur. Lord, where are the stars? Why is it so dark? Where is my breath?" He slipped into a dream.

Suddenly, the sky lit up like noontime on a summer day. Then Mike saw them—army soldiers. Thousands of them, marching past him in columns. Columns to his left and to his right. They marched from the valley up through the middle of the canyon and over the crest. They were dressed in green fatigues. Green helmets. Backpacks. Bayonets fixed on their rifles. Mike was startled by the scene, but he was more startled that none of them stopped to help him.

"Help me," he cried, but no one stopped.

"Can't you hear me?" Mike asked as they marched by. They looked neither to the left nor to the right. They appeared determined to go into a battle, a battle that Mike could not see, on the other side of the dead-end canyon.

Where is the battle? Mike wondered. *Why are they leaving me? Can't they see that I need help!*

Their pace was swift and sure. Each movement of their march was in harmony. Mike saw a great light ahead of them. Another light flowed like a river about their feet.

"Help me," Mike cried out again.

Still no one seemed to hear him. Suddenly he heard a vehicle approaching. It was a jeep. Mike could see two beings in it—the driver and what appeared to be a commander—Mike was not sure. The jeep paused. Of the driver, Mike could see only his back, for he did not turn his head. The driver kept the engine running as the commander jumped out and walked over to Mike.

The officer's eyes were like flaming light, his face noble and squared in appearance. He was dressed in full army uniform. He looked kind as he knelt down toward Mike and removed his helmet.

"Sir," Mike said, "I need help."

The commander said quietly, "Your help is right behind us."

Then he stood up, turned away, and climbed back into his jeep. The driver drove off toward the front of the columns. As the sound of the jeep faded away, so did the light, and the foot soldiers disappeared in the blackness of the night.

Mike was awakened by the howl of his old friend, the

coyote. He looked to see if he could still see anyone around. *It was only a dream*, he realized. *How could I have been so upset by them leaving me? It was not real, even though it seemed real. One thing I have to say about those soldiers*, Mike thought, *they were extremely determined to march into a battle.*

But was it really a dream? Mike wondered. For he felt a new sense of strength, the glow in the wick flickering back into a flame of life.

The night was still dark, though it was getting close to sunrise. Mike tried to sleep, but could not. He turned his head toward the valley beyond the canyon. On the distant mountain he saw something—lights flickering.

What's that? I'm not dreaming now. The lights were the size of pinheads.

Mike did not make the connection between the lights and his dream, but his help was coming from the same direction the marching soldiers had come. The commander was right when he said, "Your help is right behind us." And in the morning, a helicopter would fly from that same direction. Mike's deliverance was at hand!

12

Mike felt adrift, as though he were in the middle of an ocean. The Saturday morning sun inched over the mountains. Mike did not feel the cold. Time did not register. *How many days has it been?* he wondered. *Three days? Four? Maybe six?*

What kind of bird is that? Mike stared at the huge, unfamiliar bird circling above him. Mike had crashed in the Sisquoc Condor Bird Sanctuary. Condors are vultures.

Mike closed his eyes. He heard the wind moving the tree branches above him, casting their shadows upon his face. He felt no pain, just numbness. He was vaguely aware that he was passing in and out of consciousness. *If I'm not rescued today, I don't think I'll make it.* The realization did not bother him.

Suddenly he was aware of a new, faraway sound. *Voices?* he wondered. He opened his eyes.

"Help!" he called. But he heard nothing more. *I must be imagining things.* He was disappointed.

In the valley below, Wally thought he heard something.

"Wait!" He held up his hand. "Did you hear something?"

"No," the others said. "Did you?"

"Be quiet. I thought I heard someone."

But there was only the sound of the wind. "Guess

not," Wally said, disappointed. They resumed their conversation.

Now Mike heard them again. *It is voices!*

"Help!" he called out again.

"We heard it this time!" the others said.

Then Mike saw them in the valley far below. He was surprised. *Boy, they look small!* he marveled. *I'm not as close to the bottom of this canyon as I thought. They must be hundreds of feet below me.*

Mike breathed deeply. "Help!" he called again.

"Where are you?" they called back.

"Up here," Mike answered.

Mike's answer echoed through the canyon and bounced off the walls. He saw their heads moving back and forth, trying to determine where his voice was coming from. They didn't see him.

Meanwhile, Beaver 32 was flying in.

Again they called out, but Mike could barely hear them. The helicopter noise drowned out their voices.

"Bruce," Joe called into his remote radio, "we think we hear a survivor!"

"Really?" Bruce turned to Lou. "Did you hear that?"

"Fantastic!" she said.

"But, Bruce," Joe continued, "we can't hear him with the chopper here."

Lou rushed to the jeep to radio Jerry back at the search base to relay the message to the chopper pilot.

"Jerry, tell Beaver 32 to back off. We're trying to establish verbal communication with the downed pilot."

Once the chopper was out of the area, the ground crew called to Mike again.

"Are you in the plane?"

"No," Mike answered. "I am up here."

The effort to yell was too great. Mike blacked out.

"Can you hear us?" they shouted.

But all they heard were their own echoes. "We lost contact," Wally said. "Let's hike up to the plane."

"Not up this wall," another said, looking up hundreds of feet.

Wally agreed. "How about the ridge next to the canyon? We can try it single file."

"I wish he'd crashed near a freeway."

"I bet Chambers wishes the same thing," Wally said. Rocks scrambled and clouds of dust puffed around them at each step. They called every now and again to Mike. Sometimes he answered, sometimes he didn't.

Finally they reached the plane. To their surprise, Mike wasn't there. "Where is he?" they puzzled. They searched the immediate area around the plane.

"Mike! Where are you?" they called.

"Down here," he answered weakly.

"He is below us!" Joe exclaimed. "How did he get down there? He must have fallen over these cliffs."

"We'd better not go down that way ourselves," Ed responded. "We could fall, plus we would knock rocks down on him."

"You're right," Wally said. The trio went around by another route to get to Mike. Rocks slipped out from under their feet as they worked themselves down around the cliffs.

Mike opened his eyes when he heard them getting closer.

"Did you fall off those cliffs?" they asked when they reached him, pointing up the 300 hundred feet toward the plane.

"Yeah," Mike mumbled, by now not sure whether he had or not.

Then his eyes opened wider and fastened on a canteen on the hip of one of the rescuers.

"Water," he pleaded. It had been 48 hours since he'd had any.

"We can't give you water," was the answer. "You might have internal injuries. Water could damage you further. But I can do this." He unscrewed his canteen and poured the water onto a handkerchief. "Here. You can suck on this."

"Come over here a minute." Joe motioned the crew away from Mike. "We have a problem," Joe told the others. "Chambers is in no condition to use the jungle penetrator the chopper is carrying."

"Why?" Wally asked.

"He'd have to sit on a fold-out chair and hang on to the cable while being pulled up. He's in no condition to do that."

"Could we carry him to an area where the 'copter could pick him up directly?" Wally asked.

"There is no open place near here," Joe said, looking at the steep cliffs all around them.

"What shall we do?"

Joe picked up his radio. "Base camp, come in. It looks like the only way we're going to get Chambers out of here is with a Stokes litter. Have Beaver 32 pick one up. We also need a doctor."

"Roger. I'll notify Salinas to contact Beaver 32."

"It sure would be nice if we could talk directly to the helicopter ourselves instead of having to go through Salinas," Bruce remarked as Lou called Salinas.

"That would save time," she agreed as she started the communications relay process. In order for the crew at the crash site to contact the helicopter, the message had to go first to base camp—that was Bruce and Lou—to be relayed to the Salinas search base, and then finally to Beaver 32. Beaver 32's response had to go back the same way.

"Roger," McCourt responded to the request above the noise of the helicopter engine. "We'll fly to Santa Barbara to pick up the litter. Tell Goleta Hospital to have a doctor wait at the airport for us."

"Also," McCourt continued, "if we're going into that canyon for a pickup, we'll need the area clear of brush."

"Roger, Beaver 32," Jerry replied, back in Salinas. "I'll notify the ground crew."

Once the ground team got the message, they started

clearing the area, chopping down the tree that had stopped Mike.

Dr. John Dorman, a Navy flight surgeon on reserve, was on duty in the emergency room when the call came. He was used to this. While stationed in Vietnam, he'd flown many missions with the sea-air rescue unit from the USS aircraft carrier *Yorktown*. Dr. Dorman dressed in flight gear and was on waiting at the airport when the Huey landed.

"Sergeant House," McCourt instructed a noncom, "rig the litter to the hoist. We'll get out of here once Dorman is aboard."

As House attached the Stokes litter to the cable, Dorman jumped aboard and they took off. Miles and House filled the litter with splints and blankets as they flew up through the mountains.

"I see the plane!" McCourt called as they approached the crash site. He maneuvered the helicopter into the box canyon, to a spot far below the Cessna 150. Carefully he nosed the chopper into the corner where Chambers and the ground crew waited.

"Boy, it's tight in here!" McCourt worried.

Dowd nodded. "Hope the blades don't clip the walls!"

"Now!" McCourt shouted. Miles and House shoved the loaded litter out the door and lowered it to the cleared area below. McCourt struggled to steady the chopper against the buffeting gusts of wind.

On the ground, Joe grabbed one end of the litter. "Get the other end," he shouted to Ed and Wally above the noise of the Huey. They wrestled the litter to the ground and disconnected the cable.

"Let's get out of here!" Hands clenched tightly on his controls, McCourt lifted Beaver 32 out of the canyon and away from the gusty winds.

"That was close!" exclaimed McCourt to Dowd.

"Yeah!" Dowd shouted back. "Those blades couldn't have been more than six feet from the walls! And the wind! Did you see that Cessna rocking back and forth?"

"Sure did," McCourt answered. "Looked as if the plane could work itself off the shelf and crash down on top of us!"

Dowd was worried. "Maybe the fellows down there could make an overland carry to a safer pick-up spot."

"That's a good idea," McCourt responded. "I'll notify Salinas."

"Base camp to ground crew," Lou said on the radio. "Salinas says Beaver 32 wants you to carry Chambers out."

"Why?" Joe asked. The other two tore marker panels into strips to tie splints to Chambers broken limbs.

"The chopper's blades came too close to the side of the cliff. Also, they're worried about Mike's plane. It doesn't look too stable."

"OK, Lou, we'll discuss it."

The three looked around. "I still don't see any good spot close by," Wally remarked. "If we have to take him down to the valley, we're going to need more help."

"I don't know," Joe said, shaking his head as he looked at Mike. "I don't think he'll survive an overland carry."

"I agree," Wally responded. "And to get more help up here and get him down to a safe pick-up, we are talking 12 hours of time. The helicopter can't even land at base camp. If Beaver 32 doesn't do it, I'm afraid Chambers will be a goner."

Lord, Joe prayed silently. *Help.* He slipped his radio off of his belt.

"Base camp."

"Go ahead," Lou answered.

"We don't think Chambers can survive an overland carry. He needs medical attention now."

"OK, Joe. We'll inform the pilot and see what he decides. Stand by."

"Roger."

"What do you think?" McCourt asked Dowd. A man's

life hung in the balance. But maybe other lives too. It was a heavy decision.

"Let's go in!" Dowd answered.

"OK, Salinas, we'll do it. Have the ground crew get ready. We're coming in!"

"Great!" shouted the ground crew when they heard of the decision.

"Thank you, Lord," Joe said as he prepared Mike for extraction.

"Let's get Chambers onto the stretcher," Joe said to the others. But first they had to apply splints. So they wouldn't have to move Mike unnecessarily, they dug tunnels under him to pass the ties through. Rocks tumbled from underfoot, then rolled to the ledge 20 feet away and dropped 300 feet. The men heard the echos of falling rocks reverberate throughout the canyon.

Once the splints were securely fastened, the men rolled a green military blanket lengthwise. They moved Mike onto his side, placed the rolled-up blanket against his back, and laid him down again. A little more tunneling along his other side, and the blanket was pulled through. Then one man held the litter at a 45-degree angle next to Mike while the other two lifted him slightly with the blanket and eased him onto the litter.

"OK," Joe said, "now we tie him in and pad his head with blankets."

That done, they carried him a short distance to the clearing and radioed for the chopper to return. As the three checked Mike, they heard the chopper coming.

"Here we go again," McCourt said, taking a deep breath. He edged the chopper into the corner of the canyon, closer and closer, fighting the buffeting winds created by its own blades.

"Look at that Cessna rock!" Dowd exclaimed as the chopper passed it on its descent to Mike and the ground crew. Dust and dirt flew. "The way the winds are rocking that plane—," he left his thought unspoken, but visions of a big fireball filled his imagination.

"It doesn't look good," McCourt agreed. Drops of sweat broke out on his face. They descended to 50 feet above the clearing.

"OK, Miles," McCourt shouted into the intercom. "Lower the hoist!"

"Yes, sir," Miles said, pressing the switch to start the cable down. House and Dorman kept a close watch on the rotor blades as they churned five to ten feet from the stone wall.

Mike opened his eyes and saw the huge chopper hovering above him. As he felt the winds blowing down hard on his face, he closed his eyes.

Feels like I'm going to be blown off! Mike thought.

Miles knelt on one knee in the chopper, his left hand on the hoist cable. The trio below grabbed the hook at the end of the cable and attached it to the smaller cables from the stretcher. Then they stood back as Beaver 32 lifted the litter with Mike in it.

At first the litter hung steadily. But as the wash from the rotor buffeted it, the litter started to swing. The higher the litter was raised, the wilder it swung, in ever widening circles. The careening litter threw off the helicopter's center of balance, and the chopper blades tilted dangerously close to the canyon wall!

Miles dropped the hoist controls and lay on the chopper floor. He reached outside and grabbed the cable with both hands in an attempt to stop the swinging. House took over the hoist controls, winching Mike up as fast as possible.

Looks like we're going to buy the farm! Dorman thought as the blades edged closer and closer to the canyon wall with each swing of the litter. Of the hundreds of chopper flights he had survived in Vietnam, none had brought him so close to death.

The chopper dove toward the cliffs, then backed off at each swing. No maneuvering on the part of the crew seemed to help. Unwelcome thoughts of dropping Mike flashed through their minds. All of them, plus Mike and the men on the ground, could be killed if those blades hit.

The hoist cable was equipped with an explosive device that could instantly sever the cable in an emergency. *Why doesn't McCourt arm the device?* Dorman wondered. At that moment, almost as if he could read Dorman's thoughts, McCourt armed the device. Dorman was relieved. From Bluff Camp, Bruce and Lou watched through their binoculars and prayed.

Somehow, McCourt managed to stop Mike's swinging by catching it in the right position in relationship to the chopper. But at the last moment, while they were still fighting to control the swinging and hoisting Mike up as fast as they could into the chopper, the stretcher suddenly turned crosswise. Mike's face smashed into the understructure of the chopper, breaking his nose. He felt a sudden rush of fresh blood down the sides of his face and neck.

He opened his eyes to see what he hit. A huge steel bar pressed tightly against his face. It was one of the Huey's landing rails. Strapped in, Mike could do nothing to push himself free. With the stretcher snagged, the hoist itself stopped working. House dropped the controls and helped Miles pull Mike in by hand.

"Need a pain shot?" Dorman asked.

"Yeah," Mike mumbled. "My nose hurts." After the shot, he passed out.

It took 20 minutes to fly Mike to Goleta Valley Community Hospital, the only local hospital with a helicopter pad, on the west side of Santa Barbara. But after reaching the hospital, Mike's fight for life was just beginning.

CHAPTER

13

Civil Air Patrol spots wreckage in Los Padres Wilderness area!" the car radio announced. Ann Louise's secretary, Linda, was on her way to Los Angeles to church. "The downed plane is identified as that of Mike Chambers, the pilot missing since Thursday. No word yet on a possible survivor."

I wonder if Ann Louise knows this. Linda turned around immediately and headed back toward Riverside.

When Ann Louise's colleagues learned on Friday morning that Mike was missing, they immediately surrounded her with their love and concern. They took turns staying with her, so that she would have constant companionship and not have to wait—and meet the probable outcome—alone.

Donna and Ann Louise were eating breakfast when the doorbell rang. "I'll get it," said Donna.

"Could you step out here for a second," Linda said, backing away from the door.

"What's up?"

"Does Ann Louise know they've spotted the wreckage?"

"No!" Donna answered.

Ann Louise came to the door.

"I heard on the radio that they spotted the plane," Linda reported, "but no word yet on Mike." She was careful not to use the word "wreckage."

Ann Louise rushed to the radio and switched it on. "What am I doing?" She turned it off and dialed the rescue center.

"Yes, they've spotted the plane from the air. Chances are good that the pilot survived. It looks like the windshield is not even broken. The ground party should reach the site any moment now. We'll keep you posted."

Ann Louise sank into a chair.

More friends arrived. Jerilyn brought a casserole. Mrs. Turner handled phone calls.

Mike's sister, Debby, called from Santa Barbara. "We're on our way. We'll call you when we're halfway to see if there's any news."

A church pastor whom Mike and Ann Louise had never met called to offer support. "I appreciate your offer," Ann Louise said, "but friends are staying with me."

Ann Louise's dad, who'd been on a business trip, had finally been located; he called her. "Hang in there, honey," he encouraged.

And then *the* phone call.

"This is Elaine, Mike's flight instructor. They've reached Mike. He's alive. He's got a broken leg."

"Praise God," Ann Louise said, her eyes blurring.

"Terry and I are going to fly there. We'll be leaving about noon. That's an hour from now. If you'd like to go with us, you're welcome to come. You may not feel like flying right now, but think it over. I'll call you back in half an hour for your decision."

"Mike is alive!" Ann Louise exclaimed. "He has a broken leg!"

She ran upstairs to pack. Jerilyn helped.

"He'll probably need another pair of pants in case they had to cut off his jeans," Ann Louise said. "I won't need much. We'll be back home soon."

Ann Louise put Mike's things into a duffel bag.

"Yes, Elaine. I'd like to go to Santa Barbara with you."

Ann Louise's friends gathered around her. Jerilyn and Mrs. Turner pressed money into her hand.

"I'll stay here for a couple of hours to answer phone calls," said Mrs. Turner.

Bill and Marit Aldrich drove Ann Louise to FlaBob. "We can bring your car to Santa Barbara when you're ready," they volunteered.

Elaine was buttoning down the oil-stick cover on her plane. "We're ready for takeoff. The flight will last about an hour."

"That's better than a three-hour drive," Ann Louise said.

"You can take the back seat. Terry will be out in a minute."

Terry emerged from the small office and climbed aboard. Elaine climbed in herself and started the engine.

They taxied out to the runway and took off. It seemed strange to Ann Louise. *These are the same mountains Mike passed Wednesday*, she thought.

Elaine put the plane on automatic pilot and turned around to talk. "Mike called Terry late Thursday afternoon. He was worried about time. So when he didn't arrive that night, we thought he had decided to stay over and return Friday."

They landed at the Santa Barbara airport about 1:30. After taxiing and parking the plane, the three walked into the flight desk office.

"What hospital might an accident victim be taken to by helicopter?" Elaine asked the secretary behind the counter.

"Do you mean the plane crash? The rescue helicopter landed here a couple of hours ago for supplies."

"Where would they have taken him?"

"It would have to be Goleta Valley Community Hospital. That's the only one with a helicopter landing pad."

She picked up the phone. "I'll check."

"They're expecting him there, but he's not off the mountain yet," she reported.

"This is the pilot's wife," Elaine said, "We need to get there. Can you call us a cab?"

"I'll take you there myself," the secretary replied.

Ann Louise was quiet on the way to the hospital. *It's been three hours since they reached him*, she thought. *I thought he'd have been down long before now. And even have his leg in a cast.*

"I'm taking you to the rear of the hospital," the secretary said. "That's where the emergency room is."

The three entered the emergency entry of the one-story hospital.

"Is Mike Chambers here yet?" Elaine asked.

"No," the nurse said. "He should be here soon. You can wait in the courtyard. It's private there."

They walked down the hall. "This must be the courtyard," Elaine said. They sat down to wait.

"Are you hungry?" Terry asked. "I'll see if I can find us some sandwiches."

She returned shortly with sandwiches from a vending machine. The sun was hot in the enclosed space.

"I wonder what's taking so long?" Ann Louise worried.

"He's been exposed for two days. They may need to stabilize him a bit before bringing him down. It may even be the type of helicopter where he'd be in an outside basket," Elaine speculated.

Ann Louise began to feel forebodings about Mike's condition. A broken leg hadn't sounded too bad.

"What's that?" Terry said. Suddenly they heard the chopping sound of a helicopter; it seemed to be flying right over the hospital.

"They're here!" Elaine said.

They jumped up. "Where do we go? Where does it land?"

Elaine stopped a nurse in the hallway, who directed them to the front of the hospital.

A crowd was gathered at the entrance. They'd been waiting for some time and were eager to see the victim.

Ann Louise could hardly get through.

"This is his wife," Elaine explained, opening a way for Ann Louise through the onlookers. A crowd of reporters, with cameras running, stuck microphones in Ann Louise's face.

"What do you think of flying?" they asked.

"I flew here in a small plane myself," she said distractedly. Her attention was on the helicopter, which was landing on the circle of lawn in front of the hospital. The women reached a police barricade.

"Stay back, please!" the officer said, as the crowd surged.

"Let her through!" someone said. "It's his wife!"

The policeman let them through. They watched as Mike was loaded onto a waiting gurney and wheeled away from the copter. They stopped next to her.

"You can talk to him. He's conscious," an attendant told her.

Ann Louise was shocked at Mike's appearance. *He looks dead*, she thought to herself. His eyes were closed. His open mouth was filled with gravel. His face was completely covered with caked blood, as was the front of his sweater. *But even a small scratch can make quite a mess,* she thought optimistically.

"Mike," she said.

He opened his eyes. He was groggy and struggled to find her. "Honey, is that you?" A rush of warmth filled his soul.

She leaned over and kissed him.

"Elaine is here too," she said.

Elaine stepped forward.

"Sorry about your plane," Mike said. The reporters heard that comment and included it in all their stories.

"Don't worry about that," Elaine said. "It's insured. It was ready for an engine overhaul anyhow."

The attendants rushed him through the hallways into the emergency room at the rear of the hospital. The first thing they did was to cut his clothes off.

"Could you cover me up, please?" he asked.

"You're doing a great job," he told the nurses. "You should get a raise."

Ann Louise waited again in the courtyard as the doctors examined Mike to determine the extent of his injuries. Finally Mike's doctor called Ann Louise in. "You can see him now."

Again she was shocked by his appearance. Even with the caked blood washed off, he still looked bad. His face was covered with lacerations.

"Well, Mrs. Chambers, he missed a few bones, but he's in remarkably good condition, considering his ordeal. No organ injuries, but he broke his right leg, both lower arms, his nose, his right ribs, and the little fingers on both hands. He shattered his left shoulder into a jigsaw puzzle. He shattered his right ankle into pieces. He also broke his back in three places."

As he cataloged Mike's broken bones, Ann Louise started to get dizzy. Just as her legs crumbled beneath her, friends eased her onto a nearby cot.

"Are you all right?" A nurse passed smelling salts under her nose.

"Mike will need surgery, but we'll wait till Monday for that," the doctor told her. "We'll keep him in intensive care over the weekend to stabilize. He's lost a lot of blood. His hemoglobin is low. He's dehydrated. We don't want any surprises."

But they were surprised. Mike's light banter in the emergency room fooled the medical staff into thinking he was better off than he really was.

14

Like a knocked-out prize fighter coming to, Mike opened his eyes. Ceiling lights flashed by. The wheels of the gurney carrying him from surgery bumped over the joints in the tile floor. Pain shot through his body. His eyes blurred. He passed out.

When Mike came to again, he was back in the intensive care unit (ICU). Everything was still a blur—except for his dad's face. Mike focused on that and was comforted. He felt like the child he once was, when his all-powerful dad could make everything all right.

That was the only memory Mike had from Monday, when he underwent nearly five hours of surgery, till Thursday.

During those days, Ann Louise visited him in the intensive care unit every two hours for the ten minutes she was allowed. Otherwise, she waited in the hall outside ICU, at times with Mike's mother and younger sister, Debby, and at times alone or with others whose loved ones suffered inside the same unit.

A crisis arose within hours of Monday's surgery. During one of Ann Louise's short visits, she was accompanied by Mike's mother and a local Seventh-day Adventist minister. Ann Louise felt drained.

"He'll make it," Mike's doctor had assured her.

Good, Ann Louise thought, *but he looks as if he is dying.*

Mike was barely conscious. His eyes were closed. The skin on his hands was yellowish and bloated, like surgical gloves filled with water, stretched almost to the bursting point. Bottles suspended from poles at his bedside were connected to him with tubes and needles like a plumber's nightmare. He looked a lot worse than he had when he was first brought down from the mountain.

The doctor had said that Mike had no internal injuries, and yet a tube coming out through his nose from his stomach oozed blood into a large bottle on a pump machine.

Why? Ann Louise asked herself.

She trusted that the doctor knew what he was talking about. There was nothing else to be done. But she wondered.

"Water," Mike murmured.

"What?" Ann Louise asked, leaning forward. "Sweetheart, we can't hear you. What do you need?"

"Thirsty," Mike whispered. He could not drink, so Ann Louise spooned ice chips into his mouth. "Do you think his color is changing?" asked his mother, breaking the silence.

"It is hard to tell," Louise replied.

Mike's face was covered with lacerations and stitches. There was a T-shaped brace on his nose and across his forehead. He had several days growth of beard.

"His face does appear to be getting darker," Ann Louise said. *Should I tell the nurse?* she wondered. *I have no medical training. But he is his my husband!*

"Mike's color doesn't look good," she told a gentle-looking nurse.

The nurse accompanied her back to Mike's cubicle. Glancing at him she said casually, "You'd better go now. It's time for his X-rays."

No sooner had they left ICU to resume their vigil in the hall than they saw hospital personnel rushing down the corridor, some pushing machines. They all went into ICU.

Is that for Mike or someone else? Ann Louise wondered.

As the activity continued, Ann Louise reminded herself of the doctor's assurances that Mike would be all right, even though his condition was very serious.

It was three hours rather than the usual two before Ann Louise was allowed to see Mike again. When they did let her in, they gave no explanation for the delay. But as she approached his bed she saw an oxygen mask covering his face.

"Your husband had a shocked lung," the nurse told her.

"What's a shocked lung?" Ann Louise asked a doctor later.

"Oh, we lose a lot of them that way," the busy doctor answered, hurrying away.

A shocked lung is indeed usually fatal. Interstitial fluid builds up in the lung as the result of trauma. The lung becomes so filled with fluid that it is a solid mass. At this point, the air drawn in cannot interchange with the alveoli. There is no expansion of the tissues. The patient appears to be breathing, because the diaphragm keeps pulling air into the lungs, but the oxygen itself is not transported to the tissues to be exchanged with carbon dioxide. The skin gets darker and bluer. Death follows shortly.

The procedure for correcting this problem is to put a tube through the chest to suction out the fluid. Timing is critical—a matter of minutes.

As Mike's mom and Ann Louise watched his face grow darker, he was suffocating before their eyes. Their observation and action directly saved his life.

Mike was in ICU a week longer; then he was transferred to a regular patient room in the hospital.

"How's the pilot?" Two faces new to Mike leaned over him.

"Bet there's one guardian angel with broken wings! I'm Bruce Gordon and this is Lou Dartanner. We had something to do with your rescue."

Mike had undergone another operation on his right

ankle; it was set with a pin. Both forearms contained metal plates to hold his broken bones together. With his right leg and left shoulder immobilized in splints and casts, he had to lie on his back, unable to roll onto either side lest his back not heal correctly.

"Here are some get-well greetings!" Lou dumped a thick bundle of cards onto Mike's lap. "A lot of people followed your ordeal and rescue on radio," she said, "from as far away as Alaska and Colorado. In fact, they encouraged the pilot and spotter of the search plane looking for you."

Bruce and Lou described to Mike and Ann Louise their part and that of the others involved in his rescue. "Out of 16 small plane crashes in California last year, you're the only survivor," Lou said. "In fact, in the 25 years our local unit has been in existence you're the only pilot we've found alive."

One part of the rescue was particularly intriguing: the identity of the pilot who called in Mike's emergency signal.

"That call was the turning point," Bruce said. "With that information we were able to pinpoint our search efforts. And time was critical. Without the call, we may have found you in another day or so, but it would have been too late."

"I'd sure like to thank the pilot for reporting it," Mike said. "Who was it?"

"Well, Mike, that's a mystery," Bruce replied. "We don't know. We've tried to track him down, but the sheriff at the substation who took the call said that all he heard was a voice over the radio. No identification was given, just a voice over the air telling your location."

Mike looked up in amazement. "What about the N numbers on his aircraft? Surely he would have given those!"

Bruce shook his head. "Nothing."

CHAPTER

15

Three weeks passed. Mike's doctors said he was stable enough to be transferred to a hospital closer home. Ann Louise arranged for an air ambulance to transport him, and a physician friend, Jim McNeill, flew out to accompany Mike on the plane trip to Loma Linda University Medical Center.

Mike was at the medical center two months, plus several in-and-out visits. To see him today, he looks as if nothing had happened to him. He walks and moves around like anyone else. But he still suffers pain from his injuries.

Mike would like to fly again, but Ann Louise is not too fond of the idea. A few months after Mike's accident, Elaine and Terry sold their flight school and moved north.

Mike retrained to be an optician, and graduated in that profession from Crafton Hills College. He worked briefly in the ophthalmology department at Loma Linda University Medical Center, but working eight hours a day for five days a week proved too much. His back pain intensified to the point that it numbed his left leg. His personality changed as he withdrew into the pain, which occupied more and more of his attention. His doctor suggested he explore other career opportunities.

Mike became involved in radio ministry, with the help of Roman Rybczynski. As a radio speaker, he shared with his listeners his experiences and what he had learned about God's character. Later, Roman and Mike orchestrated the expansion into television of the Gospel in Symbols ministry. This program is broadcast all over the United States and Canada on the Three Angel's Broadcasting Network. Mike works behind the scenes as an assistant director.

A friend asked Mike what he'd learned from his ordeal.

"An agnostic friend of mine visited me in the hospital and said something that even many Christians believe," Mike replied.

"What was that?"

"He said, 'If God was really with you, He would have pushed the plane over the ridge instead of allowing you to crash.' "

"What a thing to say!" Mike's friend responded. "Of course, God was with you. You were rescued out of the canyon and are here to talk about it."

"You just proved my point," Mike said. "You and he assume that God is with us only if something good happens. If I'd died up there, wouldn't God have still been with me?"

"That's a good point," his friend answered. "Of course, God is with us regardless of the outcome of the situation. Is that the lesson you learned?"

"Yes," Mike answered. "But there's more. It's easy now to say God was with me because I was rescued, but if you were to isolate any part of my ordeal, it might appear that God had forsaken me."

"What do you mean?" his friend asked.

"Remember that second cliff? How I was hanging on and yet I still fell? I prayed with everything I had in me not to fall off that cliff! And what happened?"

"You fell off!" his friend answered.

"I sure did. I was broken up before the fall and broke more bones after. Things went from bad to worse. That's often true in life. When hard times come, it often seems to get worse instead of better. We Christians pray for God to deliver us, but sometimes nothing happens except more pain and suffering. We feel forsaken."

"How true," the friend said. "I knew someone who couldn't understand why God allowed his pain and suffering, so he left God."

"When I prayed and still fell off," Mike continued, "it really looked as if God had deserted me. But nothing could have been further from the truth. God was with me. We all have our own personal cliffs. Yet we'll be rescued from this earth in the end. Along the way we may be broken, bruised, and battered, but God is still with us."

"That's comforting," his friend said. "But how do you handle the question, why? Why does a God of love allow pain and suffering?"

"I don't even attempt to answer it," Mike said. "I don't understand any more than you do. But I don't have to understand everything for me to know that He is still with me."

"If it were easier to understand," Mike's friend said, "so many wouldn't leave God when times get tough."

"I had a lot of time to read the Bible when I was in the hospital," Mike replied. "I came across something very interesting."

"What was that?"

"In John, chapter six,* Jesus fed a multitude of people, after which they came back to Him for more food. He refused to give it. Then He said, 'I am the bread of life . . . Whoever eats My flesh and drinks My blood has eternal life, and I will raise him up at the last day.' When Jesus said that, they all left Him, saying, 'This is a hard saying; who can understand it?' "

"What is the point?" his friend asked.

"The point is that when Jesus turned to His 12 disciples and asked, 'Do you also want to go away?' Peter answered, 'Lord, to whom shall we go? You have the words of eternal life.'

"Peter and the others didn't understand Jesus' words

at that point. But where else could they go? There are things I don't understand either, but like Peter, I also say: 'To whom shall I go?' Only God has the words of eternal life."

Mike had hit upon an important point. God loves each of us. And He promised to never leave us alone, regardless of what trials we go through. For it is written in Romans 8:35, 39: "Who shall separate us from the love of Christ? Shall tribulation, or distress, or persecution, or famine, or nakedness, or peril, or sword?"

Then Paul goes on and answers: "Nor height nor depth, nor any other created thing, shall be able to separate us from the love of God which is in Christ Jesus our Lord."

Jesus reassures us in John 16:33: "In the world you will have tribulation; but be of good cheer, I have overcome the world."

Also it is written in Psalm 23:4, 6: "Yea, though I walk through the valley of the shadow of death, I will fear no evil; for You are with me; Your rod and Your staff, they comfort me. Surely goodness and mercy shall follow me all the days of my life; and I will dwell in the house of the Lord forever."

---

*Bible texts in this chapter are from The New King James Version. Copyright © 1979, 1980, 1982, Thomas Nelson, Inc., Publishers.